P9-CIW-425

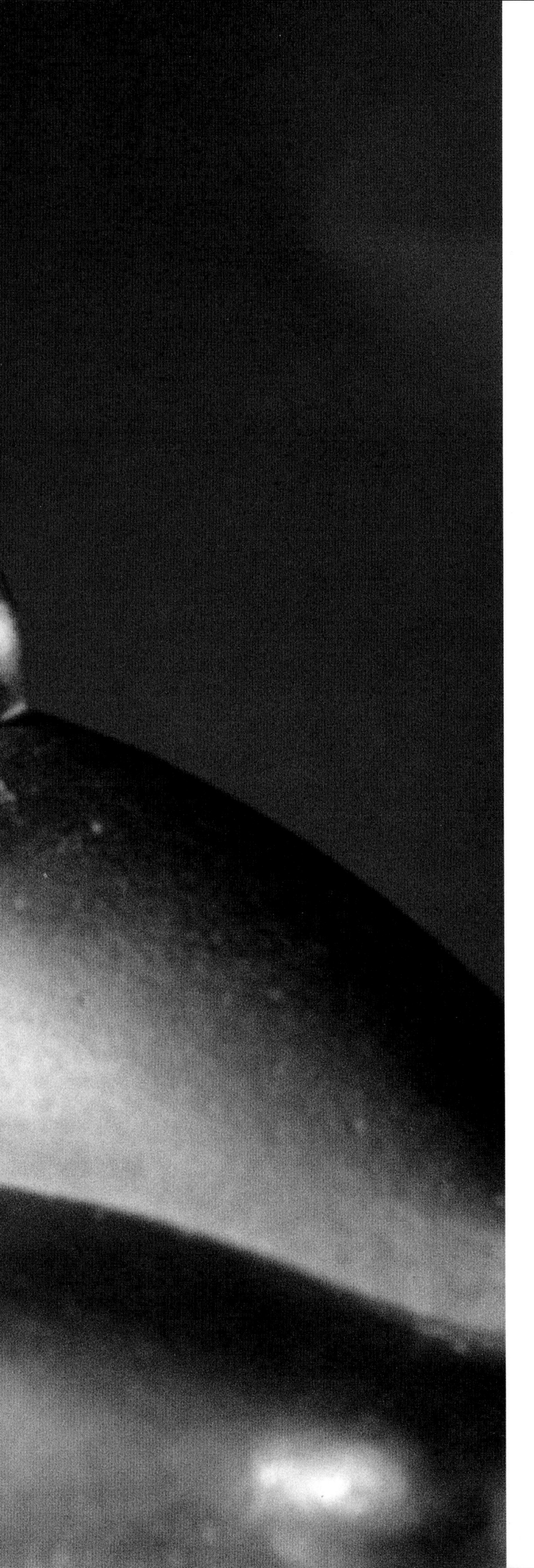

L A C H A I S E

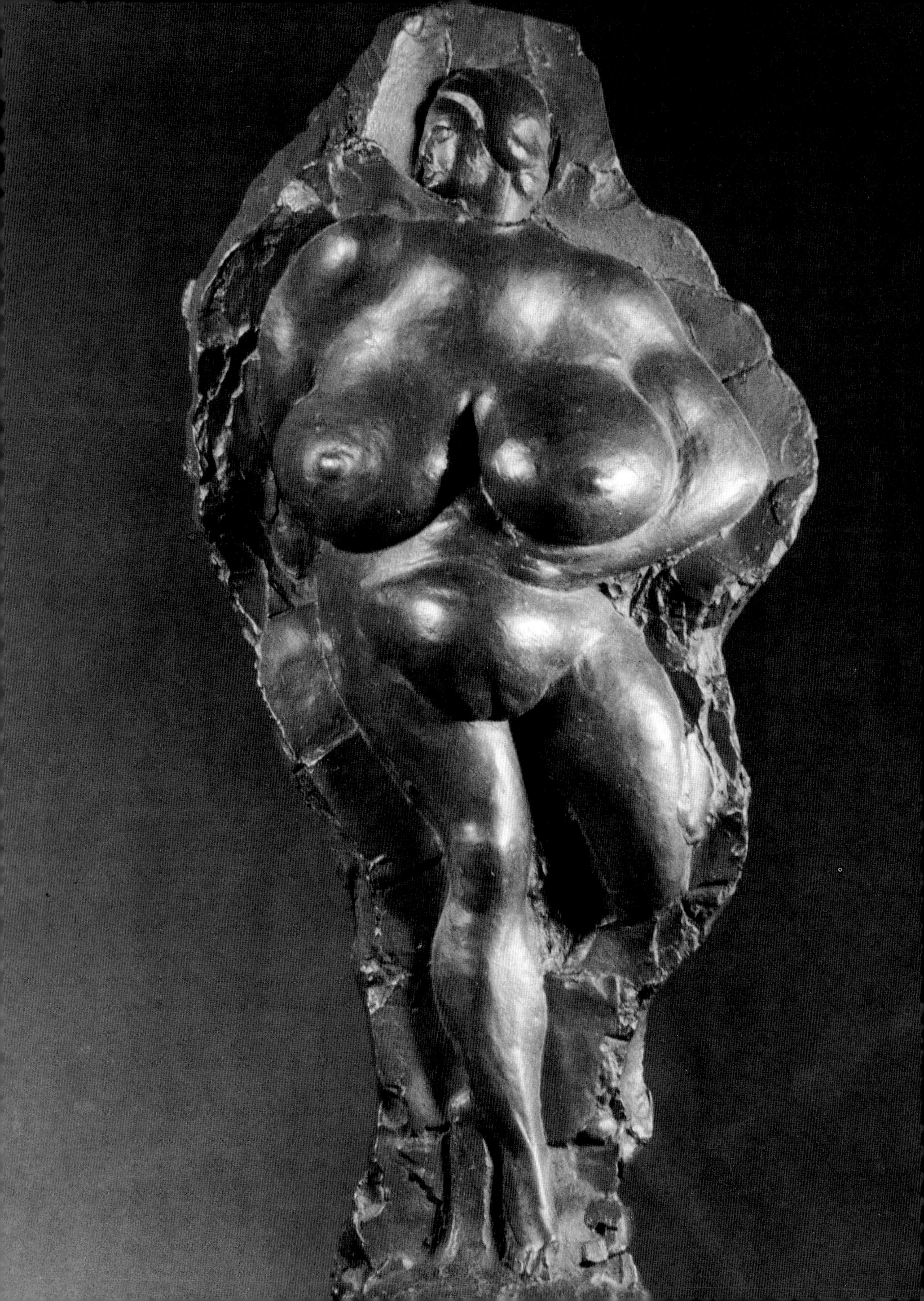

LACHAISE

Text by

SAM HUNTER

Photography by

DAVID FINN

CROSS RIVER PRESS
A Division of Abbeville Press
NEW YORK LONDON PARIS

Designed and Produced by Ruder•Finn Design

Front Cover: Gaston Lachaise, *Head of a Woman,* 1923
Back Cover: Gaston Lachaise – Photograph by Paul Strand

Library of Congress Cataloging-in-Publication Data
Hunter, Sam.1923-
Lachaise / by Sam Hunter: photographs by David Finn.
p. cm.
ISBN 1-55859-562-7
1. Lachaise, Gaston, 1882-1935 — Criticism and interpretation.
2. Women in art. 3. Nude in art. I. Finn, David, 1921-.
II. Title.
NB237.L26H86 1993
730' .92—dc20 93-10173
CIP

Inquiries should be addressed to Abbeville Publishing Group, 488 Madison Avenue, New York, NY 10022. First edition.
Printed and bound in Japan by Toppan Printing Co., Ltd.

The Sculptures

CONTENTS

The solitude called sculpture,
of Lachaise, does not date;
never describes; cannot pretend.
Once within its clutch,
we everywhere encounter
nothing archaic, nothing modern,
nothing unexperienced –
everywhere we find ourselves
conjugated by a mind which deals freely.

– e. e. cummings, 1928

For an artist who died nearly sixty years ago, leaving behind a handful of discriminating and devoted admirers and just a few public exhibitions that were ambivalently received, Gaston Lachaise today reveals an unsuspected vitality and is still causing strong public reactions with his art.[1]

Perhaps even more today than in 1935 – the year the Museum of Modern Art gave him a wide-ranging, one-man exhibition – Lachaise and his dramatic, highly personal sculpture are news once again. For example, when a selection of his sculpture went on view in early 1992 at Salander-O'Reilly Galleries, the Guerrilla Girls declared him a misogynist and rewarded the Manhattan gallery with a bunch of bananas.

THE PASSION OF GASTON LACHAISE

Protests were immediately registered by Barbara Rose, whose essay in the exhibition catalog linked Lachaise's idiosyncratic female nudes with "a voluptuous mother goddess who is neither madonna nor whore, but an abundant, generous fertility and creation symbol,"[2] and from contemporary sculptor Louise Bourgeois. She explained his obsession with "Woman" in all her aspects as his reverence for his "one god. And it was a woman, his wife . . . [in Lachaise's words] 'the Goddess I am searching to express in all things.'"[3]

This complex Woman idol is a many-faceted subject, glimpsed only by the discriminating few before Lachaise's death in 1935, at age fifty-three. Her powerful image elicited intense commentary and controversy from the beginning, though not in all her guises. As the larger-than-life-size nude, *Elevation*, of 1912 dancing lightly on her toes and gesturing delicately and mysteriously, or as the ponderous, lofty *Standing Woman* of 1932, she is a direct, if strikingly ample, descendant of countless preceding nudes. Related both to Rodin's theatrical figures and Maillol's more controlled, classical imagery, Lachaise's Woman shares an ancient tradition.

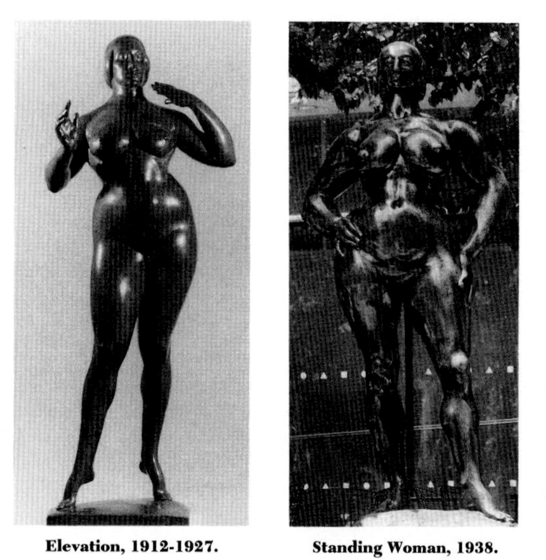

Elevation, 1912-1927. **Standing Woman, 1938.**

In much the same way, the antecedents of Lachaise's many, accomplished busts stretch back in time to the detailed realism of the Roman Republic, and even beyond that epoch to the stern, stylized figures of ancient Egypt. Translated into a bold, modern idiom through the filter of inward-turning Symbolist works—themselves inspired by the poetry that so fascinated Lachaise at the turn of the century—as well as by more recent Art Nouveau and Art Deco motifs and models, Lachaise's portraits are intense appraisals that reflect their subjects' appearances and personalities, and to a much lesser extent, his personal responses to them.

"I am a portion of the creative forces which are constantly reincarnated throughout the march of time," Lachaise wrote in 1928. "My interest in portraiture has always been keen, for a portrait of an individual is a synthesis of the prevalent forces within that individual, and in this process there is expansion for the creator."[4] He reflects the wide range of his sitters' moods and personae in his portraits. His 1924 bronze of the poet Marianne Moore, with its attenuated neck and confident half-smile, is warm and appealing; in the pure-white alabaster bust so smoothly carved in 1927, Georgia O'Keeffe is regal and distant. More mysterious and dreamlike are busts such as the 1928 lead *Mask*, an oval visage with closed eyes and cool, frozen features, and the serene *Head of a Woman* (Egyptian Head) of 1923, a sleek, submissive bronze with an exotic, otherworldly air.

As much a poetic, sculptural version of an ideal or even a vision of eternal beauty rendered in human form, the polychromed marble *Head of a Woman* belongs to a noble line of work. Carved in 1923, it is noteworthy for both its refinement and its evidence – unusual at the time – of the artist's chisel. Works such as *Mask* and *Head of a Woman* are removed from the mundane by an elegant reserve; in a sense they seem fragmentary aspects of the monumental ideals depicted so heroically and completely in *Elevation* and *Standing Woman*.

Critical reaction was largely positive to Lachaise's portraits and his graceful animal pieces and occasional large-scale commissions for such major clients as AT&T. During the 1920s and early 1930s, however, the sensitive portrait busts were what provided Lachaise with a steady source of welcome studio work. Sometimes, as in the case of his forceful portrait of patron Edward Warburg, they also provided a much-needed trip to a resort, where work continued at a more leisurely pace than his Manhattan studio permitted.

Far different in subject and intent, and for decades almost completely private, are the works that so enraged the Guerrilla Girls. These are his controversial, small studies of heavy, even grossly overweight women, only loosely based on the ample, hour-glass proportions of Lachaise's own goddess and sole Muse. They include works from the 1910s to the 1930s, among them the daring, small plaster *Nude with a Coat* of 1912, which was shown at the revolutionary Armory Show of 1913. Even more controversial was the ponderous bronze *Standing Nude* of 1921 that pointed to Lachaise's more personal, exploratory, and expressionist tendencies.

By the end of the 1920s, with his marriage and career established, but with constant effort still required to maintain his demanding lifestyle, Lachaise was exploding with creative passions that had previously been channeled into works related to his compelling conception of a mature, lush goddess. The startling, dehumanized small *Torso* of 1928 strongly emphasizes fertility while brutally, even barbarically, seeming to reduce woman to the level of an object fetish. This prophetic work led the way to even more shocking, overtly primitivizing themes, most notably his obsessive birth statement, *Dynamo Mother* of 1933, and the deeply moving, expiring female figure of his 1934 *In Extremis.*

Dynamo Mother, 1933.

With its complete elimination of head, feet, and hands and its exaggeration of breasts and pudenda, *Torso* restated Stone Age fertility fetishes, modeled after the *Venus of Willendorf.* For their time, and even for our contemporary perceptions, these two 1930s sculptures are unprecedented in their vigorous, even violent expressiveness. Sprawled in the act of parturition, with legs splayed awkwardly and nipples depicted as monstrous spikes radiating outward and upward, *Dynamo Mother* is an uncompromising image of a birth machine.

In Extremis, 1934.

By contrast, *In Extremis* clearly deals with the agony of death. Almost one with the earth – in this case, roughly worked clay – the aged, kneeling woman lies down for the last time, head thrown back in a soundless howl of agony and abandon that echoes Munch's violent *Scream* but transcends it in the sculpture's vivid, lurid three-dimensionality. Enormous, sagging breasts cascade from a jagged sternum and fall onto the ground, parting heavily to reveal the aged woman's swollen, exhausted pudenda and fleshy, withered belly. A primal icon, the subject of *In Extremis* appears to be the flip side of *La Montagne*, Lachaise's personification of Gaia, luxuriant, preening Mother Earth.

Far from the glorious, overripe fullness of the flesh in the elegant 1917 *La Force Eternelle* (Woman with Beads) or the ample *Standing Nude* of 1921, the distended and, for some, repellent sexuality of *Dynamo Mother* lacks any figment of romance, lacks even the animalism and drama of actual birth. The melting, horribly enervated flesh of *In Extremis* speaks only of the final phase of the mortal human condition, and in a strange sense, returns to Lachaise's more delicate, slim goddess celebrated in *Elevation* and various early torsos, female heads, and other exotic, reverently erotic "timeless forces of creation,"[5] and to the primal image of the great mother, Earth herself.

To the Guerrilla Girls, as to most – outside of his small circle of devoted supporters—who saw works by Lachaise during his lifetime, these idiosyncratic renditions of womanhood were nothing less than a peculiar masculine distortion, a distasteful attempt to subvert accepted canons of beauty and taste. Neither Venuses nor Madonnas, these were women long past the prime of life. Mature, voluptuous to a degree unfashionable in a period of Edwardian and flapper slimness, their well-nourished vitality and almost masculine musculature seemed offensive.

Yet, even as his more personal expressions repelled a wide segment of the viewing public, Lachaise was capable of producing work that delighted more mainstream patrons with conventional tastes and inhibitions. These more ingratiating, fashionable works include the graceful, polychrome marble *Standing Woman* (Fountain Figure) of 1927, appealingly slender in classicizing proportions as she draws a robe around her hips and gazes modestly downward, and the exquisite 1925 nickel-plated bronze study of a society lady in full regalia, *Portrait of Hildegarde Lasell Watson.*

Even during his lifetime, Lachaise's supporters were struck by the strength of the reaction against his more robust images of women, and went to pains to defend and explain him. "The cult of slenderness of 1918 found Lachaise a sort of public enemy of its thin and athletic idea," wrote Gilbert Seldes in a 1931 New Yorker profile.

Without an organ of publicity, without a press agent or the patronage of the effectively rich, Lachaise could make but one answer to his critics, an answer peculiarly proper to the artist. He replied not in words but in work. *Woman* of 1918 was followed by others; with undaunted regularity, year after year Lachaise produced a continuing line of figures, large and small, growing out of his seminal *Elevation*. Each time the new variation on that early monumental nude appeared, support developed surprisingly for its deprecated antecedent. Those who were originally most disturbed by the unabashed display of female powers in their old nemesis, often ended by declaring the antecedent truly more perfectly proportioned, grand, and compelling than the newest assault on the ideal female form.

Thus, each succeeding image of female amplitude was deemed ever more insulting, and always "indecently fat."[6] However, the more refined and flattering depictions of women, the floating reliefs and swaying socialites, as well as the polished portraits and major public commissions, earned Lachaise his reputation, and happily kept his studio empty of work, except, of course, for the more private studies that languished in plaster for years before he could afford to have them cast. But it was the more shocking revelations of the female anatomy that most satisfied and plumbed his self-expressive powers, works that today are still perceived as voyeuristic, and too literally naked and revealing when exhibited. Even now, long after the sexual revolution has been fought and won, the works he considered his most important and that received his most intense attentions between 1928 and 1935, require elaborate psychological or anthropological explanations and still cause public discomfort.

Ironically, that disjunction between one expressive pole and its opposite in his art, from his polished feminine ideal to the expressionistic virago, from the ingratiating public image to the testing private image, has created an unresolved duality in perceptions of Lachaise's oeuvre, despite his undeniable genius. But the roots of his more extreme late sculptures, with their marvelous elan vital and unapologetic eroticism, can be readily traced and historically understood. The foundation of his dynamically evolved career was laid first by his innate talent and then developed institutionally by his early facility and progress through France's national art schools. But it was a fateful human encounter in 1902 that sparked his imagination and, quite literally, inflamed his prodigious creative faculties.

He wrote in a journal in 1928: "Born in Paris in 1882, I met a young American person who immediately became the primary inspiration which awakened my vision and the leading influence that has directed my forces. Throughout my career, as an artist, I refer to this person by the word 'Woman.'"[7] That "young American person" was Isabel Dutaud Nagle, a Boston matron ten years Lachaise's senior. Unhappily married to an older man, a salesman, she was in Paris between 1902 and 1904 while her young son attended school; a photograph of Isabel from about that time shows a human version of the idealized busts that became so prevalent and obsessive in Lachaise's work during the 1920s. She gazes modestly downward, her eyes almost closed and her hair flowing romantically around her bare shoulders. Her lips are pressed firmly together, almost in a smile; her compliant pose and dreamy, withdrawn expression make her an irresistible romantic subject.

Throughout his life, Lachaise cherished the specifics of his first encounter with Isabel, known as

Belle to her family, though the rest of the world referred to her as Madame Lachaise. "One Spring day . . . as I was coming out through the beautifull formal garden and the beautifull gate of the School, I passed a majestic woman that was walking slowly by the bank of the Seine. I succeeded to meet the majestic woman later – through her the splendor of life was uncovered for me and the road of wonder beguin widening and far out reaching,"[8] he wrote in 1931, in prose still expressively French despite his status as an American citizen dating back to 1916.

Another photograph of Isabel, this one made during her return visit to Paris in 1905, shows her in a more alert but regal pose. Head erect, dark hair restrained by a bandeau headdress almost barbarian in appearance, she stares slightly downward. Her thick, long hair falls behind broad, bare shoulders and down her back, acting as a frame for her face and emphasizing the clean, strong lines of her chin. She was the inspiration for countless key works by Lachaise, including *Elevation*, which became a turning point for him, and she was described later as looking like a Lachaise sculpture with clothes on.

Even more important to the artist than her role as a model, actual or in memory, was her profound and continuing impact on his life. A few years after meeting her and becoming, instantly and eternally, in "thrall" to her, Lachaise told a friend that Isabel "has a great deal of something which it's difficult for me to express to you, something of a great calmness and ardour, a quality of both old age and youth."[9] The painter Marsden Hartley put it more strongly, referring to Lachaise's ideal of beauty: "He was always the consistent and ardent worshipper, he was always at work day and night, sleeping when the body could no longer hold out and above all this ritualist solemnity rises the figure of the indomitable pagan who saw the entire universe in the form of a woman."[10]

For Lachaise, who was the very image of the dashing young art student in his native, turn-of-the-century Paris, Isabel also represented a liberating, new cultural ideal. Even when complaining about the lack of patronage that troubled him in America decades after his fateful meeting with Isabel, he praised the vigor and expansiveness of her country: "Whenever an American artist is led to speak of his achievement in art he is, necessarily, on account of the violent intensity and fabulous wealth of this land, anchored to certain cold facts which in the United States are stressed, fantastically, beyond the reality of art . . . Financial strain from all sides, no genuine support for the better of a lifetime are yours.

"Yet it cannot be overlooked, that at present, even though neglected, the American artist 'living and true', – creative and bearer of fruit, has begun to grow roots and function in the rocky soil of America . . . This American soil is fresh. It is fertile. Flowers and fruits of new species and new beauties will come forth from it to lighten the world if some golden drops are allowed to fall in periodical, healthy showers."[11]

It is hardly surprising that Lachaise registered some qualifications regarding the generally unsupportive climate in America for contemporary art. He had been born on March 19, 1882, the fourth child of Jean and Marie Barre Lachaise; his father, a prominent cabinetmaker best known for designing the Eiffel apartment in Paris, encouraged Gaston in artistic tendencies that had emerged early. When he was five, his family discovered him happily teaching himself to carve with chisels that he had found in his father's woodworking studio.

Indifferent to books and rebellious at school, Gaston found himself drawn to nature, to flowers and trees. He got in trouble by becoming "very unruled . . . gambling wildly with marbles."[12] Two early memories that stand out in his reminiscences were to reappear in his art, transformed, though always true to the childhood emotion of wonder they evoked. He recalled "getting lost one evening among the mob at a country fair; dreadful fear to be taken by the Gypsy . . . next morning tenderly recomforted by mother teaching to me gently my name and address, this I learned quickly while standing up between her laps."[13]

More impressive was his visit in 1887 to the Cirque d'Hiver, where he saw Buffalo Bill, who represented for Lachaise the memorable spirit of wild, wide-open America. In picturesque, evocative English he described his childhood rapture as he beheld the "sumptous galloping around on a beautiful white horse and shooting down, eggs shells tosed up in the air by cavalcading Indian. These were trills to a little boy five years old – the profusion of light of music – the smell of parfum mingled with the ammonia of the stables – and also trilling – the wonderful round bossomed and round heaped lady – tossing herself up and down from a beautifully decorated big horse galloping gently in circles."[14]

Even after entering the school of "Art appliqué a l'industry – Bernard Palissy" in 1895 at the age of thirteen, Lachaise recalled his reaction to the generously proportioned women who had made such an impression: his mother with her ample "laps," and the busty, full-hipped circus rider. He studied with the school's director, the academic sculptor Jean-Paul Aubé, and with sculptor Alphonse Moncel, who became a family friend. At Palissy, Lachaise learned the basic skills and mediums that would stand him in good stead and make his methods so admirable in America: carving wood, stone, and ivory; drawing, painting, anatomy, and the history of art.

With the approval of his teachers, Lachaise skipped the last of the four years in Palissy's program and entered the Académie Nationale des Beaux-Arts; at the age of sixteen, he became the student of the conservative classicist Gabriel-Jules Thomas. "I wanted to move quickly to the Beaux-Arts," he wrote in a 1931 autobiography, noting how close he came several times to winning the coveted Prix de Rome. "This would be supreme and the dream of 'Rome' at the end of the rainbow."[15]

Talented, and widely recognized as such, Lachaise exhibited four times at the Paris Salon des Artistes Français in 1897. His realistic, loosely modeled bust of his sister, *Portrait of Allys Lachaise*, went on view despite the fact that he was younger than the rules permitted; only the recommendation of his masters gained him admission. Something of a dandy, self-assured and adorned with "long hair, sombrero and cape, wide trousers caught at the ankle, a flowing black necktie, and an encombrous cane,"[16] Lachaise later saw himself at that pivotal moment as indolent and unfocused: "For a time I remained in France lazily contemplating masterpieces of the past.

"I became unruled again. I could not stand the Grec subject any longer – and the academie requirement of the weekly nude study. I drifted to studio parties, yet not too wildly – To Montmartre . . . Le Moulin Rouge – on few occasions and for better times to The Concerts Rouges . . . Verlaine, Baudelaire, Rimbaud became my ferveur."[17]

Just at that point, only a few months after the death of his father, Lachaise met his ideal "Woman." As an American citizen of French-Canadian extraction, and an older, married woman with a child (her son Edward, born in 1893, was just eleven years younger than Lachaise), the exotic Isabel set the poetic young art student on fire. Each partner to the romantic obsession seemed like a vision to the other, and it is likely that the obstacles in their path only made them more determined to devote themselves to each other and to their love affair. In photographs of the period, Isabel resembles a Symbolist seer, a medieval princess painted by a Pre-Raphaelite; Lachaise is the romantic embodiment of the intense creative spirit, with dark eyes smoldering beneath furrowed brows.

If Isabel's proportions and anatomy prefigured the monumental, idealized sculptures of the 1910s and 1920s, and her face obviously inspired many of Lachaise's elegant, disengaged busts of the 1920s, Madame Lachaise also contributed something far more profound than appearance to her lover's work. From his first study of Isabel, a six-inch-high portrait head that he modeled within a few weeks of their meeting, to the last, his feelings about her – a clear and articulate passion – shaped the work. Yet he remembered the tiny Isabel, who weighed only about 110 pounds and stood just 63 inches high, even in stolid middle age, as "a giantess – a tremendous woman, and probably the most handsome one ever."[18]

Madame Lachaise is equally eloquent and quite as startlingly straightforward in her recollections, "He was the perfect Frenchman, yet I hated Frenchmen," Isabel later recalled. "He was so sober, nothing was ever said to hear himself say it. It was honest! He was very handsome. He had absolutely no color – very dark brown eyes, thick black hair, a firm mouth. He wore black much of the time, increasing the paleness of his complexion. He didn't like some of his photos from around 1900 because he said they were 'so frenchy.' . . .

"We shared everything. Every bit of music. We pleased ourselves as well as each other, physically, emotionally, intellectually. Neither of us had had a companion in (our) search for values and love," she recalled. "He had a reverence for women that was very wonderful. . . . He gave me a wonderful security despite the hardship. . . . He opened up another world [for me] and he said the same of me too."[19]

During the years the artist and his Muse were together, as both changed and aged, Isabel's changes were occasionally recorded with a scrupulously unflattering eye to realism in Gaston's evolving art. Already older than he by a decade, as she grew plumper and softer, he grew stouter, and more expansive artistically. "When he came to America at the age of twenty-four, he was a slender youth who had made romantic and langorous sculptures of slender youths gazing with longing and melancholy at lovely ladies," noted the 1931 New Yorker profile. "He put that behind him, and as he began to make his molded and full-bodied sculptures, his own body took on a weight which is not ponderous, and a solidity which is not stolid. Like Picasso, Brancusi, and the late Robert Chanler, Lachaise seems to have been built of one huge piece of solid rock.

"You are aware of a good skeletal structure, well fleshed. His face is ruddy, his hair straight and black, his big head is attached powerfully to big shoulders, the opposition and harmony of a round mass on a spreading base; his torso is vigorous, its supports robust and delicate. If his sculptures were all one thing, if they were all the large women which shock and annoy until they become familiar and beautiful, one would say that he was carving always the projection of himself," Seldes wrote. And he then added with some discernment, "In a sense Lachaise's statues created Lachaise."[20]

Between 1903 and 1904, Lachaise served briefly in the French Army, winning special favors even there for his obvious and remarkable artistic talents. "After a few months of doing technical drawing for an army physician I was rewarded by a leave of absence for the rest of my military service and granted a scholarship from the City of Paris," he wrote in 1931. "Life again was beautifull and more significant until my majestic friend returned to America, her home." Even with his prestigious scholarship and every hope of winning the Prix de Rome at the next Salon, Lachaise chose to leave the Beaux-Arts and begin planning for his own trip to his friend's home – and for their ultimate reunion.

Already trained in the great Beaux-Arts tradition, exposed to Symbolist poetry and art, as well as to recent, innovative works by Rodin, Lachaise entered the Paris atelier of the highly regarded Art Nouveau sculptor and designer René Lalique to earn money for his passage to America. Under Lalique, Lachaise cast jewelry, vases, and various decorative objects. Pleased to be working in the sinuous, elegant Art Nouveau style and to expand his technical repertory, he was able to draw on diverse, exotic sources that would later appear in his art. Among them are stylized forms from nature and the graceful, mysterious prototypes of the human image assimilated from India and the Far East.

Within a year, he had put aside enough for his voyage, a paltry sum of $30 in savings. It was, he later remarked ruefully, one of the few times in his life that he was able to save anything at all. In December 1905, he set sail from England, and never again returned to France. He landed in Boston on January 13, 1906, with only the most rudimentary ability to express himself in English, very little money, and an introduction to a Beacon Hill family, who provided him with a room.

Resourceful as ever, he quickly found work with a commercial sculptor, but then lost that job just as quickly when he spent too much precious time approaching his assignment, a Gothic Madonna by some accounts, angels or other funerary ornament according to others. In the traditional Beaux-Arts academy fashion, it seems that Lachaise mulled over his job too long, musing rather than getting right to work. He also may have offended his employer, who questioned the skeptical French artist's religious beliefs in angels.[21] Whatever the reason for leaving that first employer, Lachaise was soon busy in the studio of a prominent Boston sculptor, Henry Hudson Kitson, for whom he did "moulding, casting guns, cartridge boxes, flags, plaster architectural models" on one enormous commission, a Civil War memorial for Vicksburg.

Within a short time, Lachaise had established the routine he would keep for many years, both in Boston and New York. During the day he devoted himself to his employer; at night, often for most of the night, he worked furiously at his own sculpture in his modest studio. Isabel did not end her marriage until 1917, but the couple spent most of their private time together. With Isabel and on his own, Lachaise visited art galleries and museums. He also attended dance performances, later expressing plastically his admiration for Isadora Duncan and Ruth St. Denis. Already fascinated by the art of India and Southeast Asia, his interest in Japanese aesthetics was evident in Boston, where he had Japanese prints on his studio wall. No doubt he was impressed with the important Far Eastern and Egyptian collections at the Boston Museum of Fine Arts before he moved on to New York.

Kitson left Boston in 1912, relocating to Greenwich Village; Lachaise decided his chances of success were greater in New York, and shortly after followed Kitson to Manhattan. There he also began working part-time with the commercially successful Paul Manship. Soon he shifted over entirely to Manship's studio and once again found time for his own work. In his rooms he began his first life-size sculpture of Isabel. "I worked intensively both for a living – with extra hours on account of need of extra money for living and producing my own work (as required). I would work long stretches of at times 12 hours as an assistant to Paul Manship," he later wrote.[22]

Breaking new ground even before 1912, when he saw Isabel less frequently than he wished,

Lachaise began pouring his fevered, romantic passion into his art, and devoting all the free time after his job to his own sculpture. Thus he transformed his private emotions and vision into the physical substance of medium, and sculpted not the real Isabel, not even the Isabel of memory, but rather his deeper, more obsessive love and sensation of Isabel. "After my days work as an assistant [in Boston] I would work at night in a small studio of my own on my own work," he later wrote.[23] "Slowly, personal expression came out of what I was so intensely living. This is where as reverently and with all the genuine simplicity possible I will express my profound gratitude to the leading inspiration which still leads me today, my wife – the majestic woman [who] passed by once years ago on the Bank of the Seine."

There were ardent exchanges of letters with Isabel, even after they were married and living in New York, where they maintained different addresses, he in his studio, where he often spent his night in work, and she in her own apartment. The letters track the transmutation of passion into art, as hot and private as his late, expressionistic studies of life's ultimates: birth and death. "I worked from you all afternoon expressing your body – expressing your thoughts – your body is your thought. It has been burning hot in the studio – it is good atmosphere around me – I am all aflame – a flame which burns of you. The heat, the light in the studio, the work, the little slippers, the 4 corners of the studio close me in with you . . . The best of All Me all Over you In and Out."

Accepting the complications of Isabel's life, Lachaise kept busy with his work while he waited for her. They visited, took trips together; in 1907 Lachaise had his first glimpse of Maine, where they would later buy a home and the artist would devote himself to his other great passion apart from art, gardening. In 1916 he became an American citizen, and in 1917 he and Isabel were finally married in New York and celebrated their civil ceremony at a dinner given in their honor by Manship.

By then Lachaise had accumulated twenty sculptures in bronze and marble, primarily small busts, reliefs, and women in various poses, and he felt ready to show his work. He proceeded to approach a number of New York art dealers, one by one, working down a list he had carefully formulated, ending with the two dealers he considered the most desirable, Gallery 291 and the Bourgeois Galleries.

Lachaise's experience with Alfred Stieglitz at 291 was unsettling, and it would take another nine years before he chose to show with the first great champion of modern art in America. "I stepped into 291 which was very familiar to me, being there a devoted visitor, I addressed Mr. Stieglitz for the first time, asking if he would be interested to see some of my work – My question some what went wrong – bringing out from Mr. Stieglitz the argument, 'How can I know if I will be interested without having seen your work?'"

"I got impatient take my hat and left. I was, several years later [invited] to be Mr. Stieglitz guest with a one man show in the Intimate Galleries in Park Avenue. After this incident my last chance was left. I appeared at the Bourgeois Galleries – unwrapping without a word a piece of my sculpture before Mr. Bourgeois, and waited – Mr. Bourgeois looked over my think for over five minutes I managed to keep quiet – 'I like it' came Mr. Bourgeois words – 'You want an exhibition? I will come to your studio tomorrow morning and see the rest.' Mr. Bourgeois was there early the next morning on his way to his Gallery," Lachaise wrote in 1931, adding that when the exhibition date was set, he ran down Fifth Avenue to tell Isabel the great news, then rushed on to his job at Manship's studio.

For months he lived a strenuous double life, working long hours by day to support the demanding Isabel and to prepare for the upcoming exhibition, and then putting in long hours by night on his own work. "Going to 'bed' at four in the morning on a small cot in the studio," he recalled, "I would read for one hour by a glaring electric light . . . Stefanshon Life in the North, Amundsen, and Scott in the Antartic. These men were my hero, and I read them exhilerated by the comfort of my little cot, relaxing warmly until 8 at the morning – to get up again for assistant work.

"My own work began to sale – few personal very entousiasm from the beginning multiplied to more numerous collectors, they where never of the frivolous type, but very strong in their appreciation. My 'assistant' activity was eventually dropped and all of my time devoted to my own work."[24]

When the exhibition opened at Stefan Bourgeois's gallery, in February 1918, it included twenty-nine sculptures, as well as drawings. Among the works were peacocks, dolphins, sea lions, busts and small statuettes, reliefs, and the plaster version of Isabel in *Elevation*. Already Lachaise's keynote style, with its identifiable mix of elegance and sensual bravado, was emerging in his primary subject, sensibly augmented here, with decorative animal studies, which he enjoyed but considered less important than his Woman studies. In *Elevation*, the figure is unfashionably ample but perfectly poised as if weightless on balletic, prancing toes, in a harmonious, complex contrapposto that evolved in response to a variety of influences, from the Beaux Arts and Rodin to the modern dance and Indian sculpture.

Flock of Seagulls, 1924.

Rising upward from the frail base of the toes, past swelling thighs and hips to a wasp waist, and expanding again, in the pulsating rhythm of life, to breasts as full and fascinating as those that rose and fell before an entranced five-year-old at the Paris Wild West Show, the magnificent composition culminates in the face, serene and inward-looking, and the hands that gesture so mysteriously and ambivalently toward it. Not so much Isabel as the ideal object of the artist's desire, expressed iconically, Lachaise's first *Woman* is a restrained version of his lifelong obsession. Her demeanor is both submissive and aggressive, her gesture shielding and inviting; the work's mixed message echoes its disturbing blend of ancient and modern, real and ideal.

No longer young, she is nonetheless intimidating in her forceful, physical presence and composure. She is neither particularly seductive nor feminine, although powerfully female in her anatomy. She appears to be a peculiar synthesis of man and woman, perhaps of Isabel and Gaston rather than Isabel alone, stylized to conform to the artist's ideal. Indeed, throughout his career, important pieces by Lachaise look as much like him as they do like his significant other and acknowledged Muse. From the time of their first meeting, Isabel's and Gaston's profiles and compact builds seem uncannily similar. As both aged and became heavier, so did the noncommissioned figure studies. If, as many commentators have surmised, Lachaise's ultimate subject is creativity itself, the great generative forces that exist at all times and in all places, then the concept of a force made carnal, blending the lovers in Miltonian fashion and drawing from various art historical sources, must have been enormously appealing to him.

While Lachaise was known for his pleasing and arguably unchallenging commissions – elegant fountain figures, serene, allegorical reliefs, insightful portrait busts, refined figurines – it is the more personal work that he later chose to include in his ground-breaking final exhibition at the Museum of Modern Art in the spring of 1935. The positive reactions to the 1918 show at the Bourgeois Galleries, in the meantime, suggested some of the directions Lachaise's work would take over the next seventeen years, although they gave little sense of the intensity and social extremism of the work that he himself considered the most important of his career.

Later, the noted art critic Henry McBride recalled his feelings when he first saw the work of Lachaise, who would also sculpt a portrait of McBride and elicit his unwavering support through the years. "It was in a specially wakeful moment that I sauntered into the old Bourgeois Gallery of a dozen years ago and came upon the Lachaise sculptures there exposed. Whatever there was in me of Vasari sprang instantly into the quick. I felt, 'Here's business for the historian. This is great.' . . . What astonished me most with its beauty was a female nude that may or may not have been larger than life but seemed so.

"There was an air of exuberance, of exaltation, of expansiveness, about the figure. . . . To eyes that had grown somewhat habituated to the platitudinous carvings of the day the Lachaise 'Woman' was so different that at first she seemed a priestess from another planet than this. She must have been at least early-Egyptian, early-Arabian, or at least pre-Greek! But that was only at first. In a minute or two the strangeness disappeared, the authoritative satisfaction of the sculptor in his work made itself felt and a mere critic could see a beauty that though new was dateless and therefore as contemporary as it was 'early.'

"I left the gallery firmly convinced that I had seen a masterpiece."[25]

A few others shared McBride's instant, high opinion of Lachaise's genius. Among the most influential was a group of idealistic and artistic young men associated with the Dial, which during the 1920s showcased some of the best art and literature of the period, solicited from America and Europe. Lachaise had met the magazine's owners, James Sibley Watson, Jr., and Scofield Thayer, through the poet e. e. cummings (Edward Estlin Cummings), who had become a friend of his stepson Edward Nagle while both were students at Harvard. Indeed, what has become known as the Dial Group, enlightened and intellectual supporters of literature and the arts, had all attended Harvard at roughly the same time.

The Dial, founded in 1840 by the Transcendentalists, had a long and glorious history. Published in Chicago until the 1910s and providing serious critical reviews, it had shifted its focus to a radical socialism by 1919, when Thayer and Watson took over and gave it a new mission as a literary and artistic beacon of the "new." After the magazine moved to New York, it was recast and flourished once again through its talented, if opinionated, contributors. For a time, the Dial succeeded in its ambition to provide its readers with the best in contemporary culture, although not necessarily the most radically avant-garde opinions or examples.

During the 1920s, the readership never rose much above 13,000, but the distinguished writers it attracted exerted a profound influence on the literary and artistic worlds. Its contributors read like a who's who of distinguished figures in the arts, here and abroad: Sherwood Anderson, Max Beerbohm, Anatole Broyard, Joseph Conrad, Charles Demuth, Andre Derain, T. S. Eliot, Jean Giraudoux, Thomas Hardy, James Joyce, D. H. Lawrence, Wyndham Lewis, Vachel Lindsay, Henry McBride, Thomas Mann, John Marin, Henri Matisse, Pablo Picasso, Ezra Pound, Marcel Proust, Bertrand Russell, Carl Sandburg, George Santayana, Arthur Symons, and William Butler Yeats, to name but a few.

The Dial published reproductions of eighteen works by Lachaise, and no fewer than four major and several smaller articles appeared in its pages about him and his work before the magazine's demise in 1929. This influential journal, avidly read by the best and the brightest, thus anointed Lachaise one of America's most prominent artists, and certainly its leading sculptor. His relief *Dusk* became the frontispiece for the inaugural issue of the magazine, on January 20, 1920.

The importance to the artist of his Dial connection went far beyond its early recognition of his accomplishments, or its generous reproductions and flattering verbal appreciations. Equally critical were the friendships he formed through the magazine with such key patron saints as the art collector Edward M. M. Warburg, who became his most devoted individual supporter, and Lincoln Kirstein, the balletomane and art critic, whose untiring championship eventually persuaded Alfred Barr, another Harvard product on the cutting edge of New York's cultural life, to award the

Museum of Modern Art's first one-man sculpture show to Lachaise in 1935. The Dial cast a wide, intricate, and powerful net, and Lachaise was clearly its preferred artist, but that was also attributed by some art world insiders to the conservative Thayer's well-known prejudices in favor of representational art.

Not only did Thayer publish photographs of many Lachaise sculptures and rather lavish commentary on his art and give voice to his ideas, but he also included the sculptor in his intimate circle of friends. Among them were socialite artists Florine Stettheimer, Gertrude Vanderbilt Whitney, and George L. K. Morris, the "Park Avenue Cubist," who commissioned a full-length portrait of himself and one of Lachaise's most powerful and monumental works, the massive concrete *The Mountain* (*La Montaigne Heroique*), for his estate in Lenox, Massachusetts.

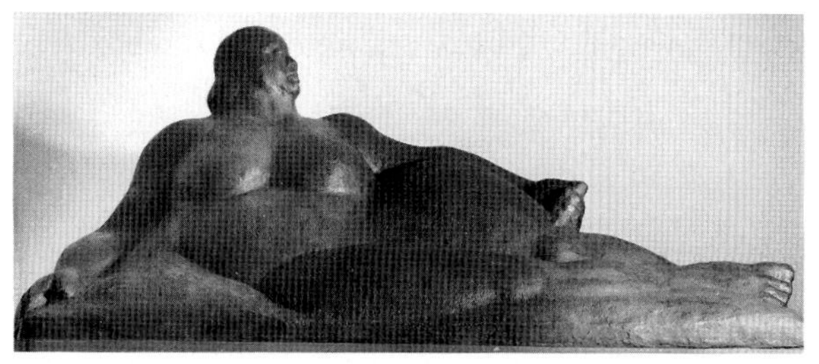

The Mountain (La Montaigne Heroique), 1934.

In addition, a number of fellow artists and admirers from his association with Stieglitz added to Lachaise's prominence, among them the photographers Charles Sheeler and Paul Strand, who took striking pictures of Lachaise and his work and artists such as John Marin, whose bust by Lachaise is generally considered his portrait masterpiece, and Marsden Hartley, who wrote gener-

John Marin, 1928.

ously about the sculptor's work. During this critical and heady period of discovery, Lachaise attracted many new collectors, among them John D. Rockefeller, Jr., and A. E. Gallatin, an affluent and public-spirited painter who had recently opened his Museum of Living Art at New York University in Washington Square.

To the chagrin of some of even these enlightened supporters, who have been described as "a small liberal elite critical of the narrow philistinism of American culture, and in particular of the inhibited, repressive spirit of Puritanism that denied the body,"[26] Lachaise crossed the line into the forbidden and taboo territory of candid sexual expression. His motives in this endeavor are complex, as he seemingly embarked on a subject matter that had only recently been excavated by science, through Freud's insights and teachings. So powerful were the forces of repression in America and elsewhere in the world, that even Barr and Kirstein reluctantly capitulated and, fearing a damaging public outcry, decided to withhold Lachaise's more private, experimental works from his Museum of Modern Art show. None of his sexually explicit sculptures were shown publicly until the 1960s, long after the artist's death.

Although some viewed his controversial late work as scandalous, a number of his closest supporters persisted in defending it as a "passionate celebration of the vitality of eros and an expression of psychic liberation from restrictive taboos."[27] Cummings, for one, wrote a fervent, honest assessment of Lachaise in the premiere issue of the Dial, priming readers for the artist's second one-man show at the Bourgeois Gallery, which opened eleven days later. The poet began by attacking anyone who did not agree with him – even those who admired the sculptor. "Lachaise has, in the past few years, made a large number of artists extremely enthusiastic, and a great many gallery-goers very nervous, not to mention the ladies and gentlemen who may have died of anger," he noted, going on to attack such respected contemporary artists as Manship and Elie Nadelman, as well as two artists revered by Lachaise, Lehmbruck and Brancusi. "Lachaise's work," he wrote, "is the absolutely authentic expression of a man very strangely alive."

Critical opinion following Cummings's estimation was quick and sharp, as was the reaction of Stefan Bourgeois, who was attacked personally in Cummings's review. After nothing sold from his second show at the Bourgeois gallery, Lachaise moved on to the C. W. Kraushaar Galleries on Fifth Avenue, which began to sell a number of his works in 1920 and 1921, and he continued to show there until 1931. Besides showing his sculpture in New York galleries and completing an amazing number of busts for clients as varied as Cummings, Antoinette Kraushaar, McBride, Marin, Stieglitz, and Thayer, Lachaise also won increasing numbers of major commissions, among them peacock sculptures for James Deering's estate, a decorative frieze for the new AT&T Building, and a life-size marble figure for the Atkinson Allen estate.

By the late 1920s, although finances remained a constant worry for him and at his most threatened moments propelled him on impulsive trips to the nearest pawnshop with an unfinished bronze or even his precious sculptor's tools, Lachaise had become an established, respected figure in the American art world. His work had entered a number of major collections, among them the Cleveland Museum of Art, Phillips Memorial Gallery, and the Smith College Art Museum. In 1922 he and Isabel bought a house in Georgetown, Maine, and began renovations. Isabel began to spend much more time at the Maine house, even holding salons there, but for both it was an important refuge from the hurly-burly of the city and an oasis of transforming beauty. By 1931 Lachaise was still maintaining a hectic pace, but he also found time to relax, often attending the burlesque with his friend Cummings. His exuberant 1930 bump-and-grind bronze Burlesque achieves a wild, almost futuristic anatomical deformation and abandon, capturing movement and attesting to his enjoyment of the kind of low-life, populist spectacle that the uniformly male, American Scene artists had so recently begun to discover and exploit.

Burlesque, 1930.

"He spends his winters with the roar of the elevated just outside his studio on West Eighth Street, and his summers in Maine," Seldes reported in the New Yorker. "In New York, he is not a frequenter of artistic circles and finds his entertainment where most other people do: at the theatre and at the movies. This winter he was enchanted by Noel Coward and "City Lights." He also has a passion for the Zoo and the Aquarium, but that may be professional. In Maine he enjoys his only mastery of a modern mechanism – he drives a Chevrolet with great enthusiasm – and works in his garden.

"He is as much at peace in one place as the other, and most of his work is done in the noise and distraction of the city. He has managed to extract quiet from its noise and solitude from its crowds."[28]

None of that quiet, and none of the distraction, are suggested in the great, penetrating works of Lachaise's final period, especially in the condensed, brilliantly focused evocations of the primal, creative urges, and at the other extreme, the extinguishing forces of nature. Transcending time and place, concentrated as if in the urgency of the need to communicate, Lachaise's balanced acrobat or buoyant *Elevation* becomes by the late 1920s a shell of her former self, fragmented or truncated, distorted or hollow. While they can be read as extensions in a sense of Lachaise's vibrant, gestural portraits of Marin and McBride, and are also reminiscent of Rodin's occasional late expressionist eruptions, the great *Floating Figure* and two 1928 bronzes, *Torso* and seated *Torso*, go even further and test the boundaries of public taste with their nightmarish

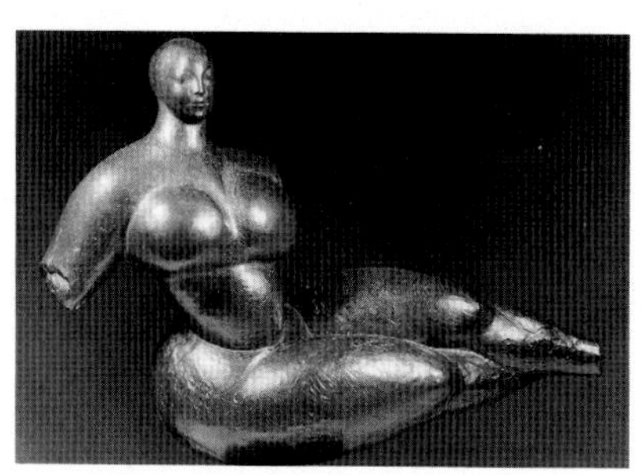
Floating Figure, 1927.

Torso, 1928.

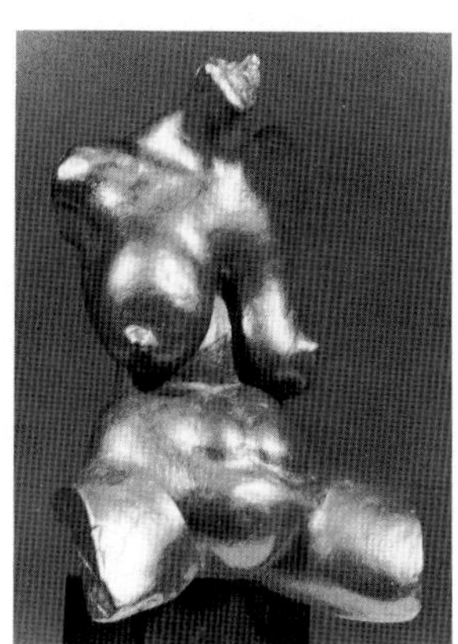
Torso, 1928.

exaggerations of female organs and their explicit sexual focus.

Marsden Hartley felt that these more liberated works were made by a "natural male . . . the indomitable pagan who saw the entire universe in the form of a woman." Although Lachaise was grateful when others appreciated his work, on whatever aesthetic or cultural grounds, the late Torsos show an obvious debt to Stone Age fertility fetishes, such as the Willendorf Venus, which the artist first saw reproduced in 1923.

It must have been a startling revelation for him: faceless, almost headless, without hands, feet, or any other body part unnecessary for reproduction, the ancient, lumpy, pitted Venus gave birth to Lachaise's last and perhaps greatest group of sculptures. Inviting, welcoming, and explicit in their enticements but never coy or lewd, the Torsos are not so much about sex or sensuality, lust or love as they are about the overwhelming urge of all living things to generate new life. Married to his only love when he was thirty-five and she was forty-five (too old to have children with him), Lachaise channeled his obsessive fecundity and generative drive into his art – subtly and appealingly at first, veiled in manly but still female form.

Throughout his short life, however, he continued to satisfy clients with pleasing, acceptably fashionable, representational works, from classicizing figures to bounding dolphins and gracefully floating, nude acrobats. But in his multifarious Woman, that primal essence, he was able to let himself go as he had done nowhere else, and as no other artist of his time could attempt to do.

Kneeling Woman of 1932–34, may appear to be an almost grotesque, cartoonish creature, crouching on the earth and gazing upward in supplication of whatever gods ruled her destiny. But *Breasts with Female Organ between, Large* is undoubtedly his most disturbing invention, unprecedented even among the surrealists for its uncensored sexual imagery. His powerful reduction of female sexuality oscillates rather brutally between expressive abstraction and a repellent realism, with an unavoidable suggestion of pain and mutilation. Nonetheless, these last works are potent, entirely memorable, visual statements about the sheer physicality of being, and the essential frailty and irrevocable ugliness of the flesh as it withers with age but refuses to surrender the indomitable human spirit.

Kneeling Woman, 1932-34.

While Lachaise was a "true artist" in Hartley's sense and estimation, he was also a "natural male," and his work was not made to please a particular woman, not, presumably, even the universal "Woman," but to let him express something deep and important in his own being, something vital and surely aggressive about how he experienced life, himself, and women in his art. The duality men so often seem to attribute to women, the "Madonna-whore" or "bitch-goddess" burden is given full, and often fearsome and full-throttle expression in Lachaise's late works. Men are uneasy with what

Woman means to them, and to humanity, according to Simone de Beauvoir, and undoubtedly have trouble dealing with these feelings.

"From the day of his birth man begins to die: this is a truth incarnated in the Mother," she says. And this resentment, in man, extends to the flesh he impregnates. "In procreation he speaks for the species against himself: he learns this in his wife's embrace; in excitement and pleasure, even before he has engendered, he forgets his unique ego. Although he endeavors to distinguish mother and wife, he gets from both a witness to one thing only: his mortal state.

"He wishes to venerate his mother and love his mistress; at the same time he rebels against them in disgust and fear."[29]

Such an uneasy, if uncompromising and honest passion, gives Lachaise's most important work its force, and makes it really impossible to ignore, whether one's reaction is as positive as Cummings's, or as appalled and edgy as that of Barry Schwabsky, writing in the July–August 1992 *Sculpture* magazine: "What impressed me most about the late work of Lachaise was the immense license he allowed himself, the liberties he took with the representations of the female body. I don't know of anything so extreme in modern art. . . . What we share by experiencing these works is not the desire for that object but rather the desire to be able to manifest one's own desire so fully, so shamelessly."[30]

Despite his average size, Lachaise was a very big man in spirit, as Marsden Hartley recalled in 1939, four years after the sculptor's sudden, brief illness and untimely death from leukemia. The French-American artist had "dark eyes, dark flowing hair, and an elemental burning in him like the flames on the hilltop of a burning city, you felt the tumult of his ardours and his idealistic ideas in every look and movement of him, he was alive with passion for art and the pure expression of it . . .

"He believed in his personal star and to him it was the most radiant of all, and he left the world outside himself to its own ridiculous or sublime devices, and it mattered not at all which it was."[31]

Isabel, Madame Lachaise, may have inflicted unreasonable demands on her ascetic, all too readily accommodating sculptor-husband, from her excessive need for material comforts to a fifteen-year wait before acceding to marriage. But as his elected Woman, she gave the sculptor permission, perhaps even the impetus that a once-indolent, rather dreamy and introspective French art student needed in order to objectify his passion and transcend the merely carnal. Inspired by the fleshly object of his desire, Lachaise translated his powerful urge to create and generate new life into enduring sculptural forms that truly do express, in his own words, "the glorification of the human being, of the human body, of the human spirit."[32]

Isabel Lachaise

Lachaise had long fascinated me as a potential subject for photographic exploration. I believed that his monumental figures (and even his small works are monumental) could be the basis for dramatic visual compositions, and looked forward to the opportunity of producing a series of photographs that would show the strength of his work. I am grateful that with the publication of this volume I have been able to do so. In a curious way, photographing Lachaise's sculpture reminded me of my experience some years earlier when I photographed the work of Antonio Canova for a book published together with a text by Fred Licht. At the time, I was captivated by what I considered the sensitive and sensuous rendering of flesh in Canova's female nudes, despite the fact that Kenneth Clark, Mario Praz and H.W. Janson had characterized Canova's figures as frigid. I later had the privilege of showing my photographs of details of his beautiful nudes to all three scholars and was gratified by their enthusiastic comments about the representation of warm, living flesh revealed in my prints.

Canova's works are, of course, at the opposite end of the spectrum from Lachaise's, and yet they both have to do with love of the human body — Canova's figures are uniquely delicate; Lachaise's are uniquely passionate.

For me, the proof of Lachaise's greatness lies in the tension of form he achieves in every element of his sculptures. No matter how exaggerated the anatomy he invents, I never feel he has gone too far.

NOTE FROM THE PHOTOGRAPHER

Even his most extreme expressions are not like caricatures one might find in pornographic literature. They are esthetically powerful forms created out of the breasts, buttocks and genitalia that to him represented the supreme ecstasy of sexual excitement. His work seems to be an expression of the elemental life-force that gives rise to the procreative urge as well as the ultimate experience of love.

Lachaise's greatness, however, was not limited to the female nude. His portraits show how his superb skill as a sculptor extended to other subjects. They are strong and vital works, projecting the personality as well as the likeness of the individuals he portrayed.

My wife and I have owned a little torso by Lachaise for many years. It is a high relief with a hollow back, and we never grow tired of looking at it. But when I photographed the sculpture for this book, I discovered for the first time that the back and sides of our torso are as finely wrought as the front. There is a tendency, I think, to look at Lachaise's sculpture only from one point of view because his images are so overpowering, but unexpected discoveries can be made by exploring his work from all angles.

The opportunity to publish this book came about serendipitously when I visited a comprehensive Lachaise exhibition at the Salander-O'Reilly Galleries in New York in the spring of 1992. I had never before seen such a large collection of Lachaise sculptures, and hadn't realized how consistently great his work was. I introduced myself to Larry Salander and Bill O'Reilly and asked if I could photograph the works in the exhibition for possible publication. They were delighted, and the results were so satisfying that they arranged an exhibition of my photographs in the gallery. I also want to thank John B. Pierce, Jr., president of The Lachaise Foundation, for his enthusiastic support of the project. I took additional photographs of Lachaise sculptures in New York at the Metropolitan Museum of Art, the Museum of Modern Art, the Hirschl & Adler Gallery, and the Nelson Rockefeller Collection at Pocantico Hills.

In photographing Lachaise's works with special lighting and lenses, I felt I was able to reveal aspects of his sculpture which had not been fully recognized in the past. My goal was to show the inner strength of the sculpture and the emotional intensity with which Lachaise imbued his forms. I hope that the selection of photographs in this book, together with the eloquent and insightful text by Sam Hunter, will enable readers to experience the full range of Lachaise's achievement, and appreciate his position as one of the great sculptors of the twentieth century.

David Finn

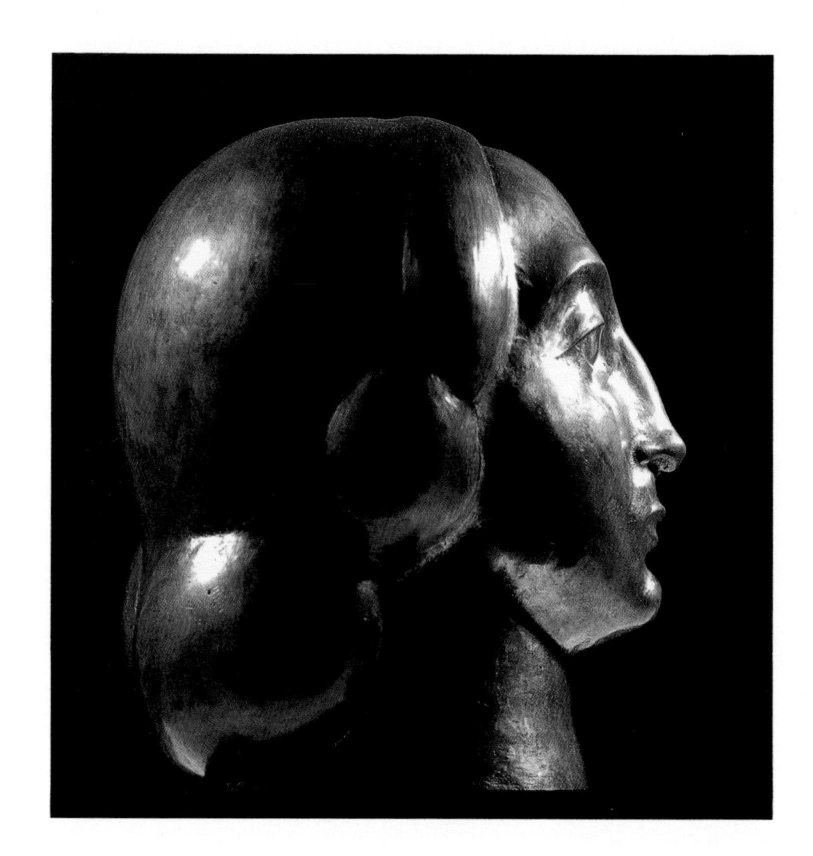

LACHAISE:

THE LIFE'S WORK

THE SCULPTURES

"Lachaise was that singular being of today and of yesterday, the worshipper of beauty, he thought of nothing else, beauty was the meat and bread, it was his breath and his music, it was the image that traversed his dreams, and troubled his sleep, it was his vital and immortal energy."

Marsden Hartley

FOETAL FIGURE/ RECLINING WOMAN *C.1910*

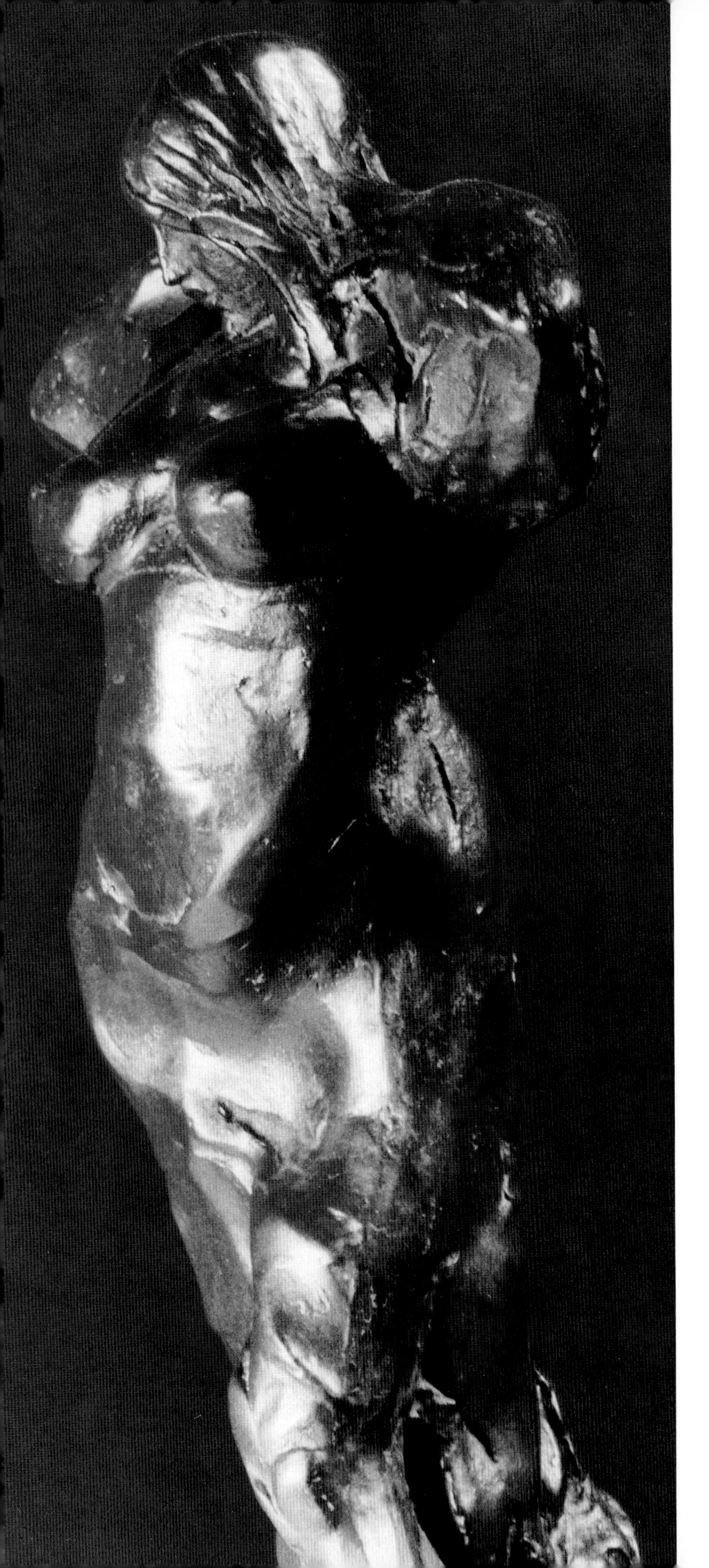

"At twenty, in Paris I met a young American person who immediately became the primary inspiration which awakened my vision and the leading influence that has directed my forces. Throughout my career as an artist, I refer to this person by the word 'Woman.'"

Gaston Lachaise

WOMAN ARRANGING HAIR
1910-1912 (left)

NUDE WITH COAT
C. 1912 (right)

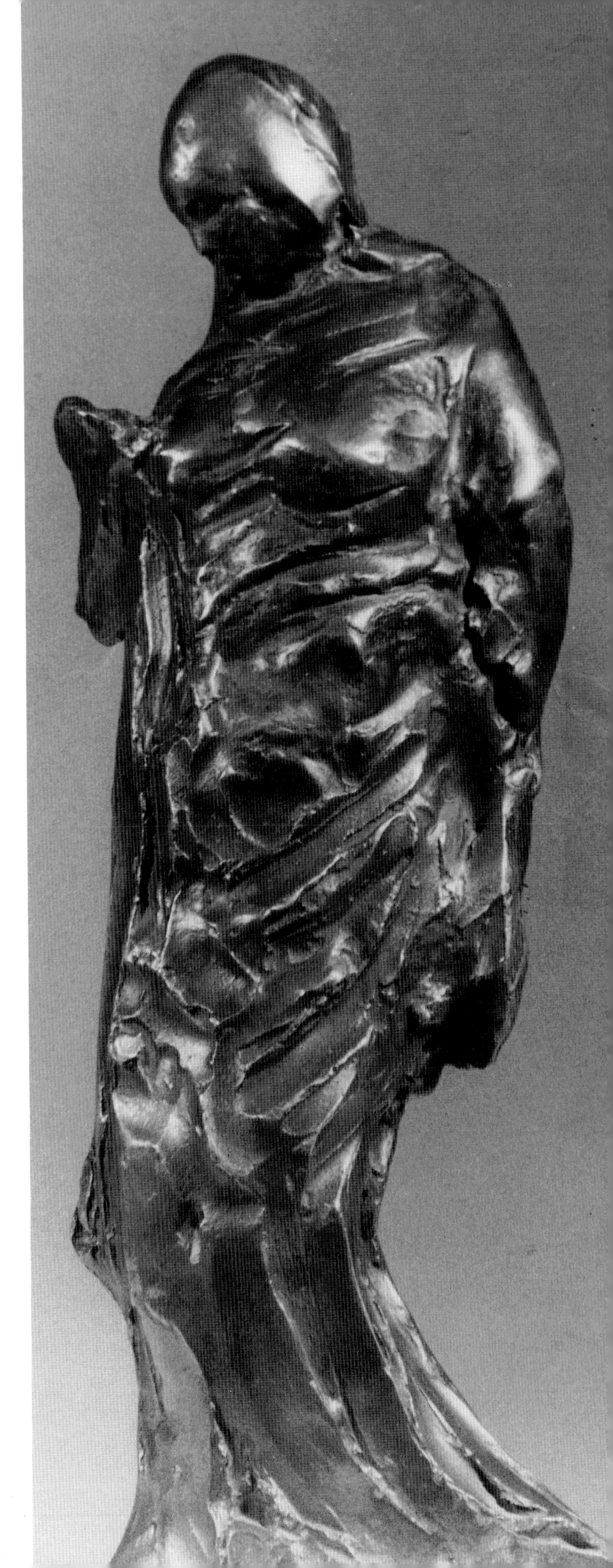

WOMAN LOOKING DOWN *1912-1914*

TWO FEMALE FIGURES
1915 (left)

WOMAN ASCENDING STEPS
1915 (right)

"In all matters of craft and artisanship, and in the tenor of sensibility that governed them, he was French. As a mature artist he has at his fingertips all the refinement and facility of technique that were once the glory of the great European art academics. Yet the maturity of his art belongs to America. It was in America that his art first came to flower."

Hilton Kramer

 STANDING WOMAN WITH ARMS BEHIND HER BACK *C. 1918*

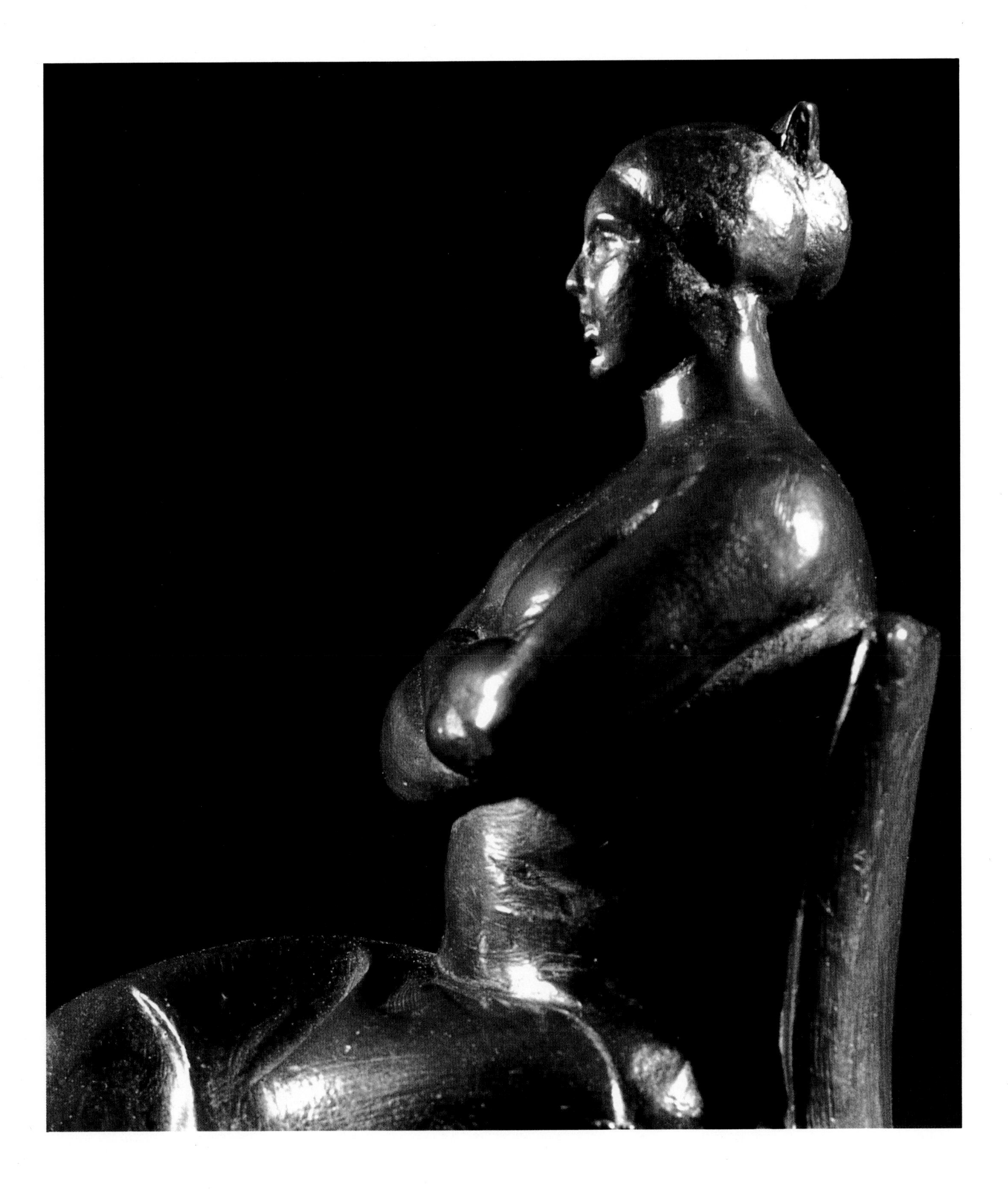

"Lachaise was unquestionably the true artist, he was the sculptor of the joyous moment... and since for him the dream was a magnificent "affair du coeur" he believed first and last in the efficacy of it, and the proud substance of beauty as a force in itself."

Marsden Hartley

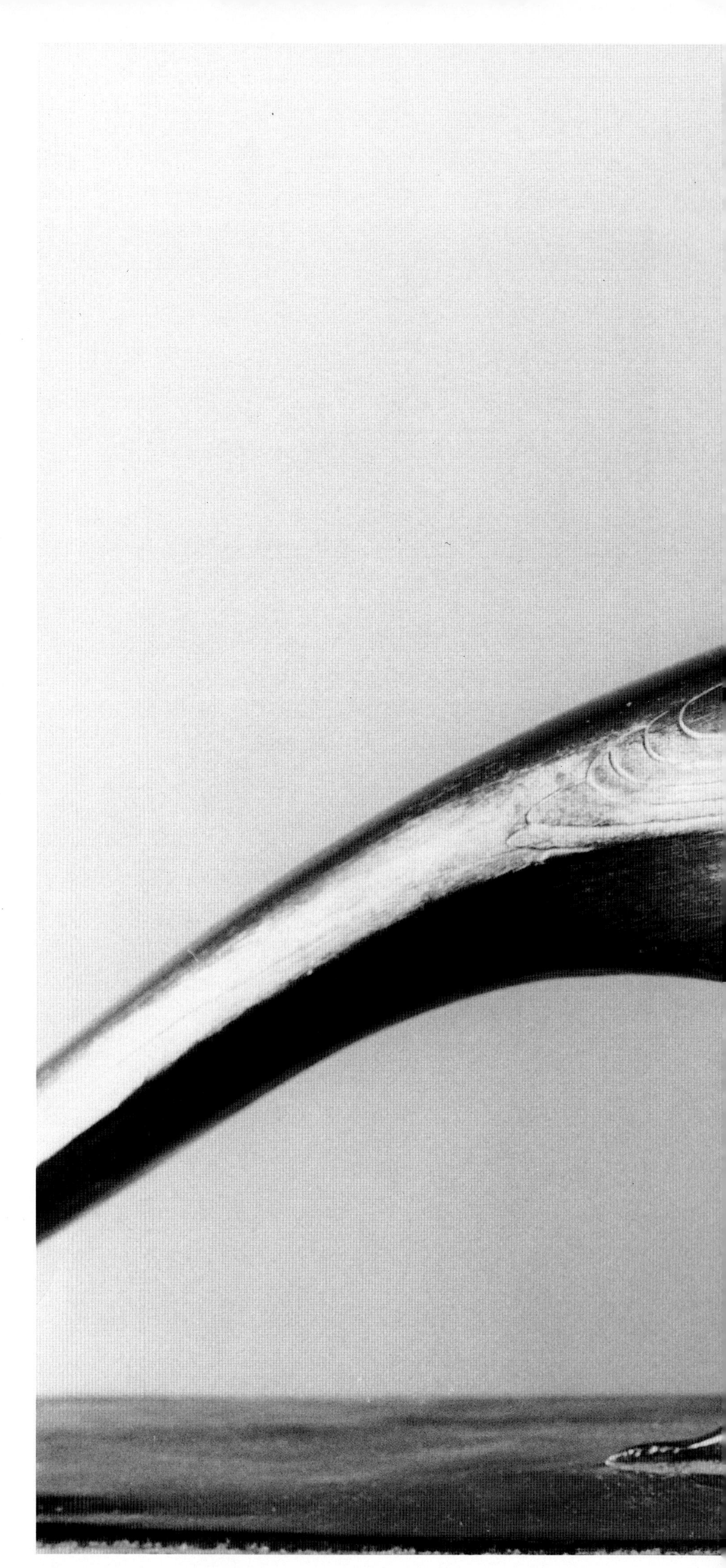

THE MOUNTAIN *1921*

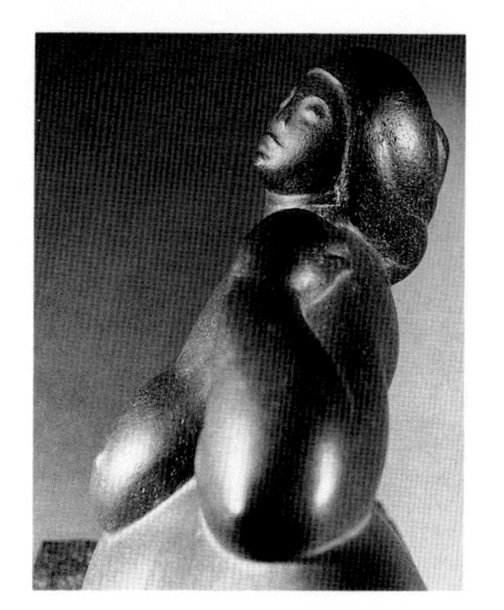

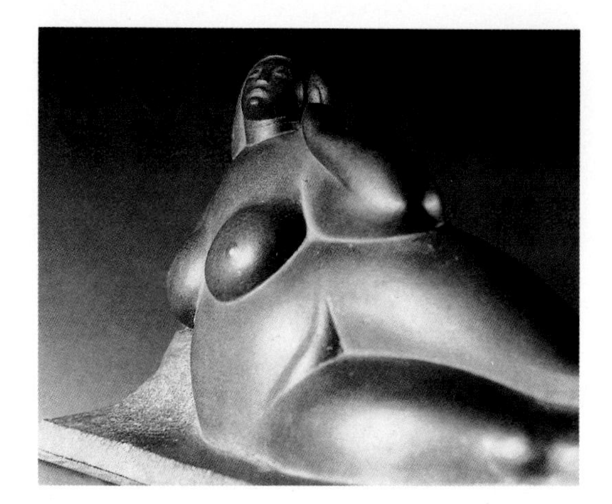

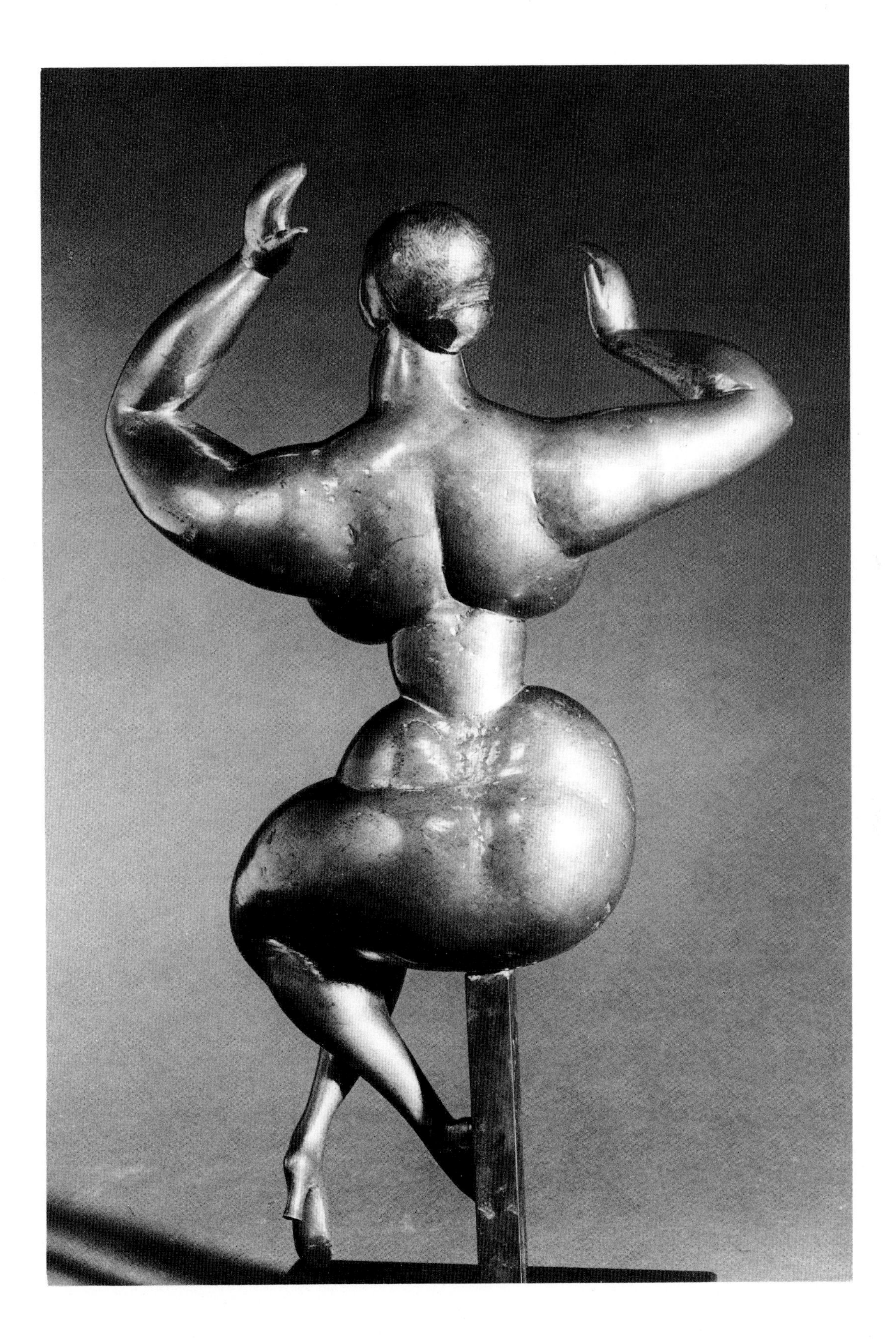

SEATED WOMAN WITH UPRAISED ARMS *1926*

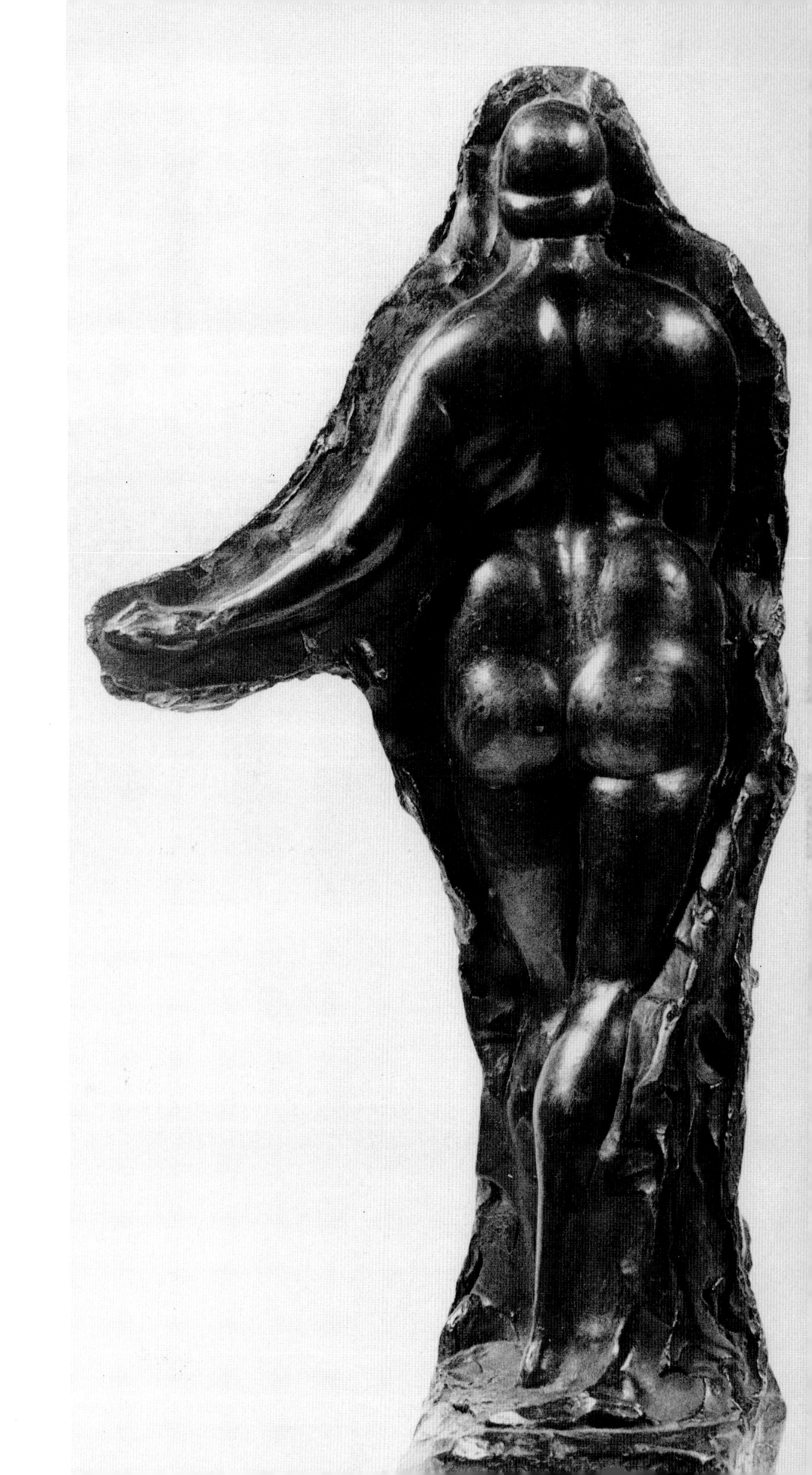

RELIEF OF THE REAR VIEW OF A FEMALE NUDE
1924

"The Lachaise "Woman" was so different that at first she seemed a priestess from another planet than this. She must have been at least early-Egyptian, early-Arabian, or at least pre-Greek!"

Henry McBride

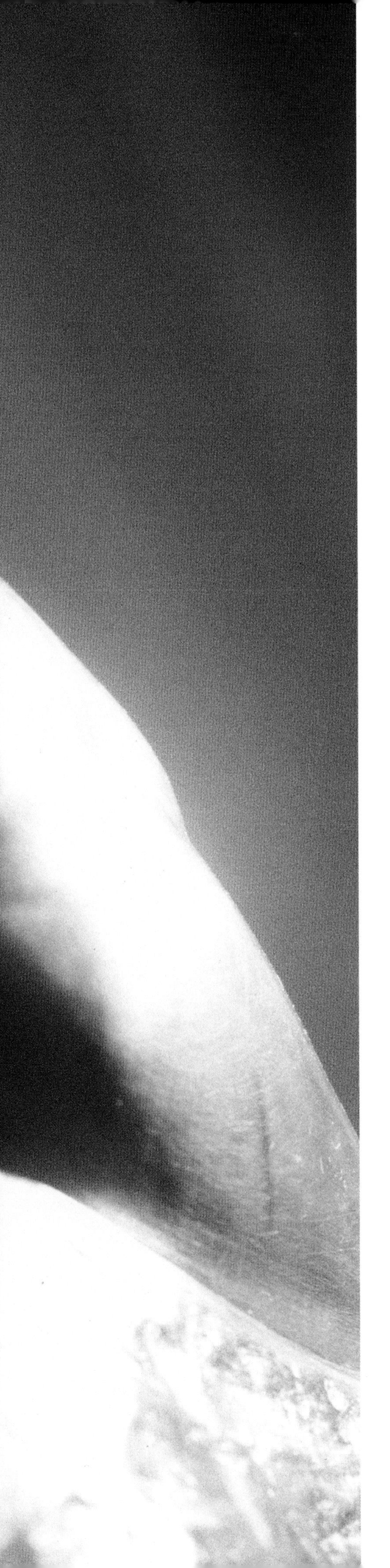

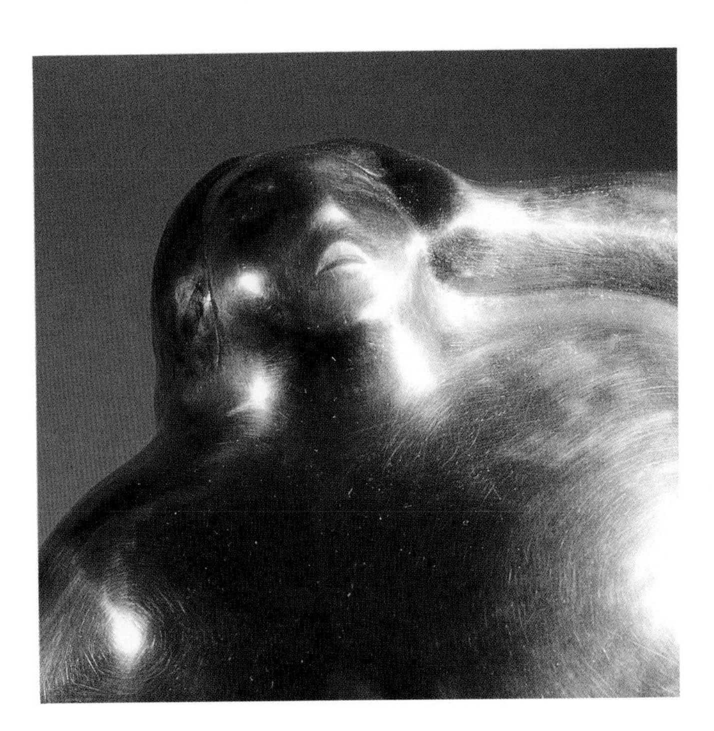

FLOATING NUDE FIGURE *1924*

"Lachaise, above all other sculptors since the Renaissance, is the interpreter of maturity. He is concerned with forms which have completed their growth, which have achieved their prime; forms, as he would say, in the glory of their fulfillment."

Lincoln Kirstein

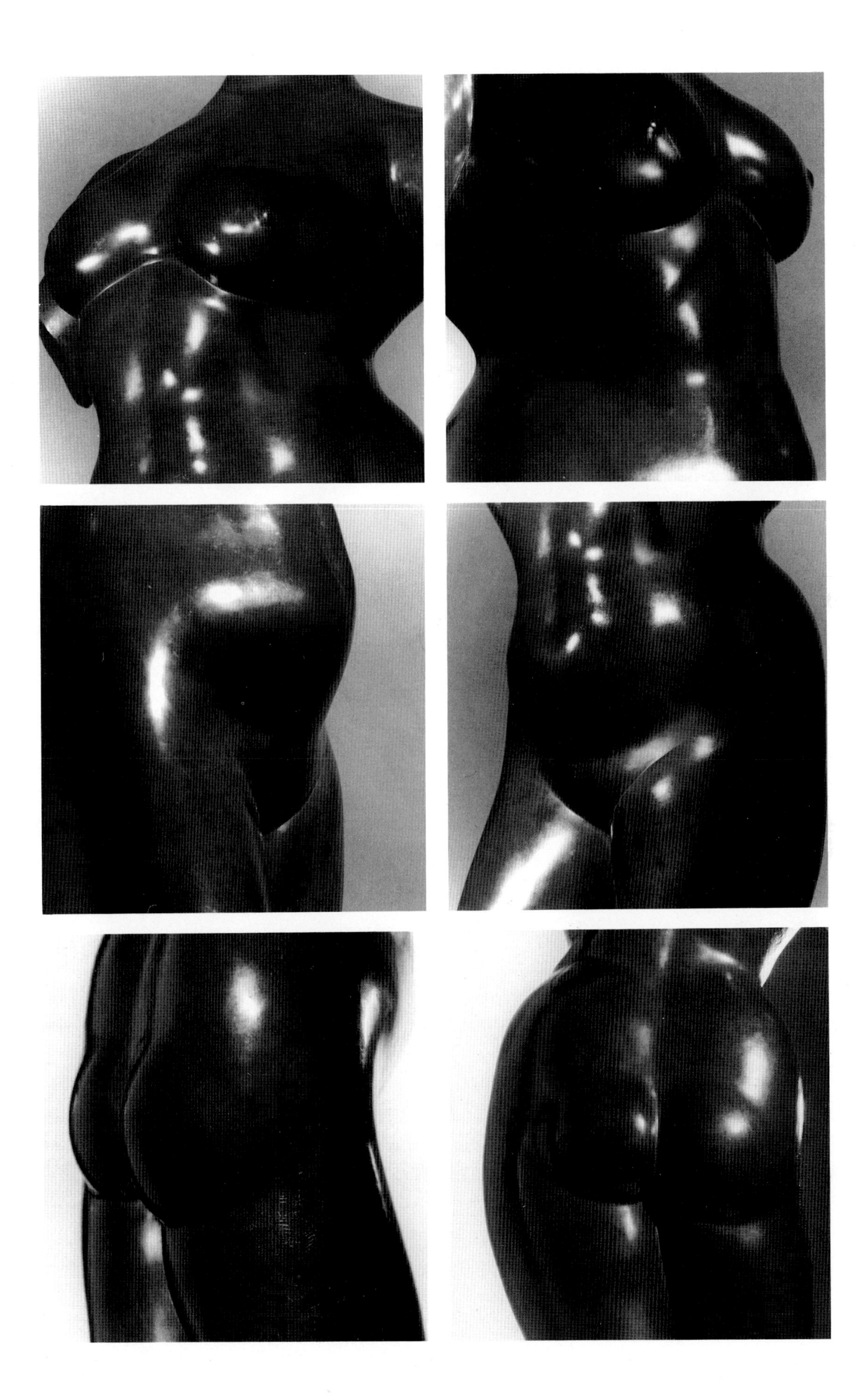

"The exquisitely varied masses—rising from the narrow, graceful feet on tiptoe to the musculature of the pronounced thighs and torso to the elegant arts that are carried, rather like a dancer's, to understated points of climax in the poetry of the hands—are a miracle of modeling in which we see Lachaise's profound technical power here imbued for the first time with his quest for a heroic image."

Hilton Kramer

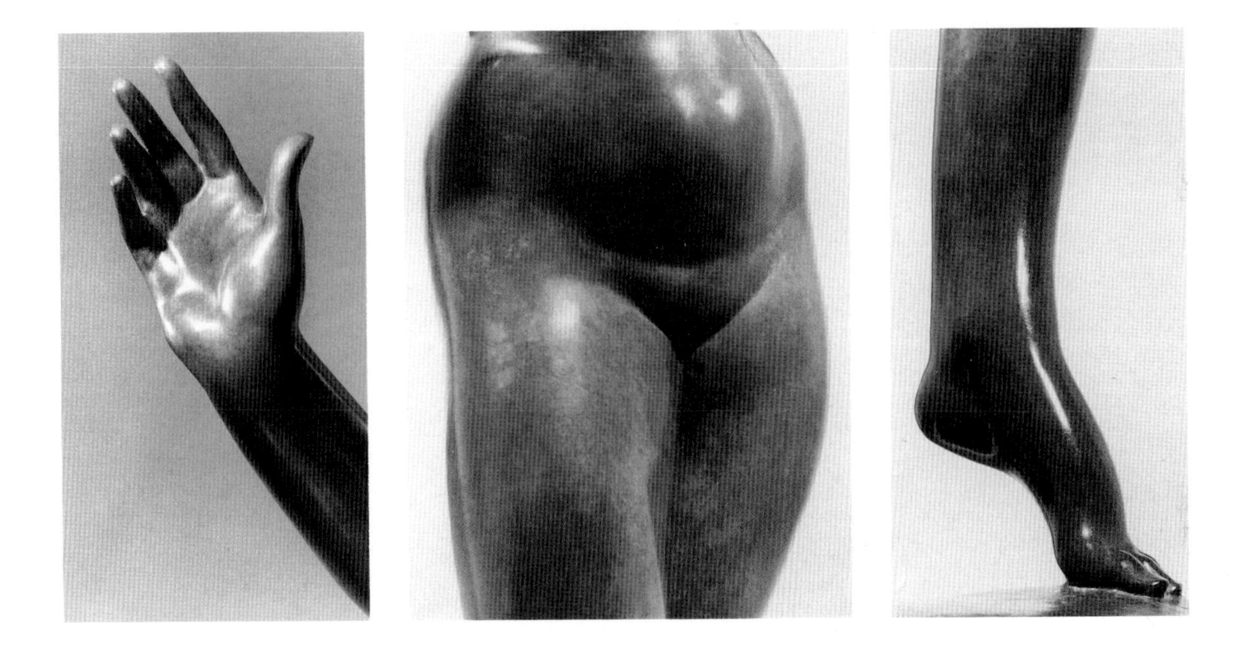

THE BIGGEST LITTLE WOMAN IN THE WORLD
C. 1918

TORSO *1927*

DANCER *1928*

"Thy time is thee to wend with langour such as gains immensity in gathering grace; the arms to spread; the hands to yield their shells."

Hart Crane

STANDING NUDE, LEFT HAND RAISED *1927*

STANDING NUDE *C. 1927*

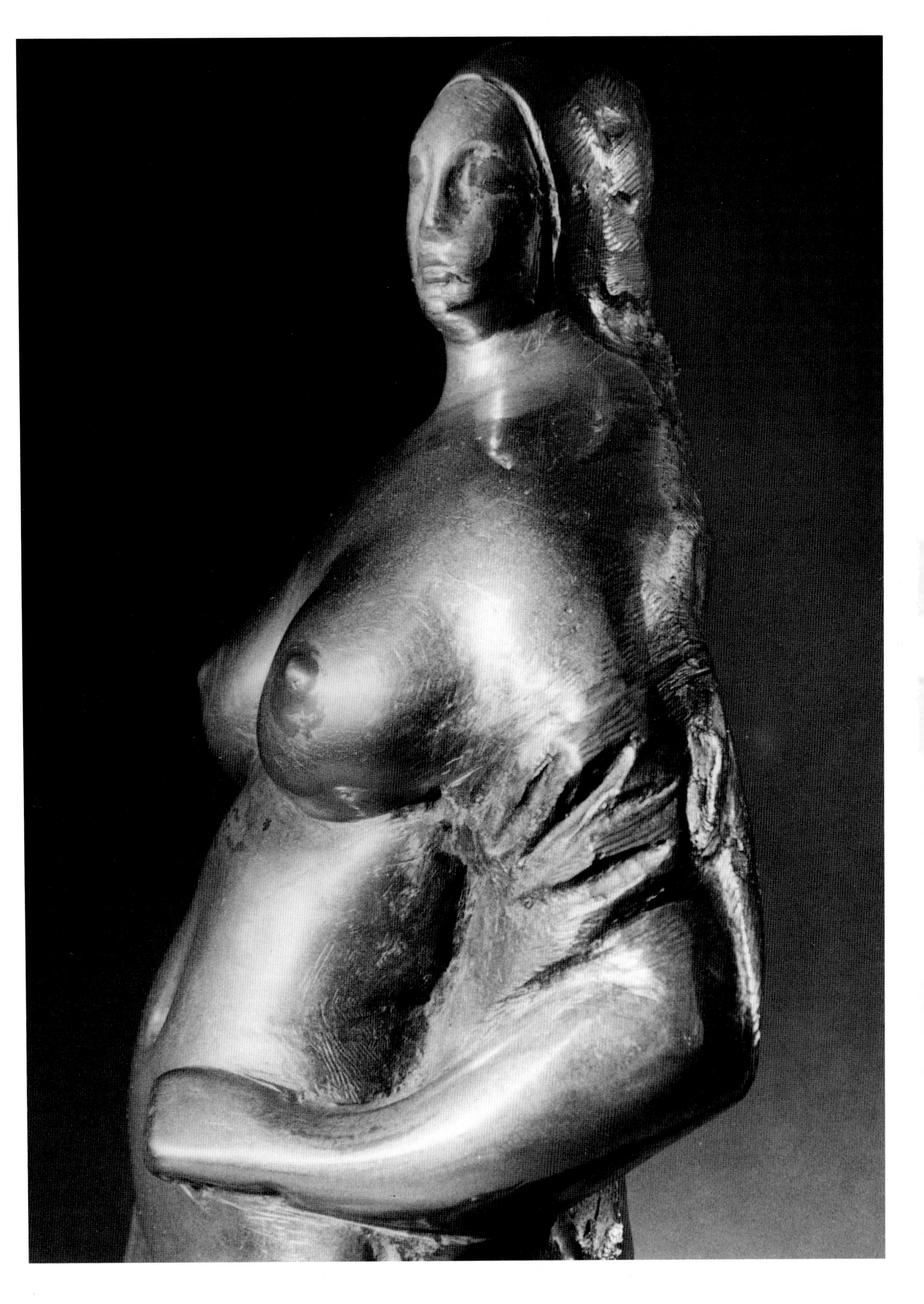

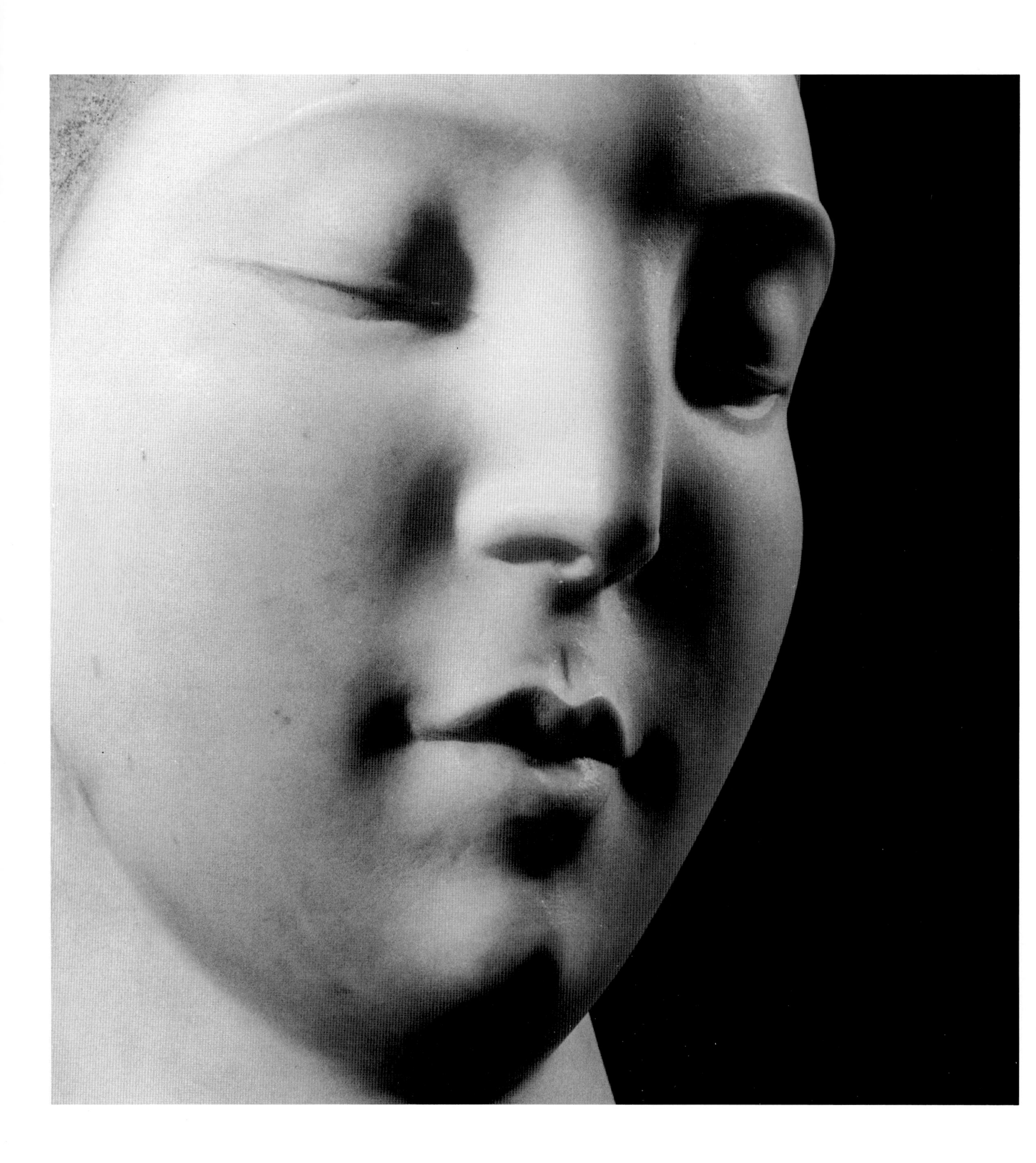

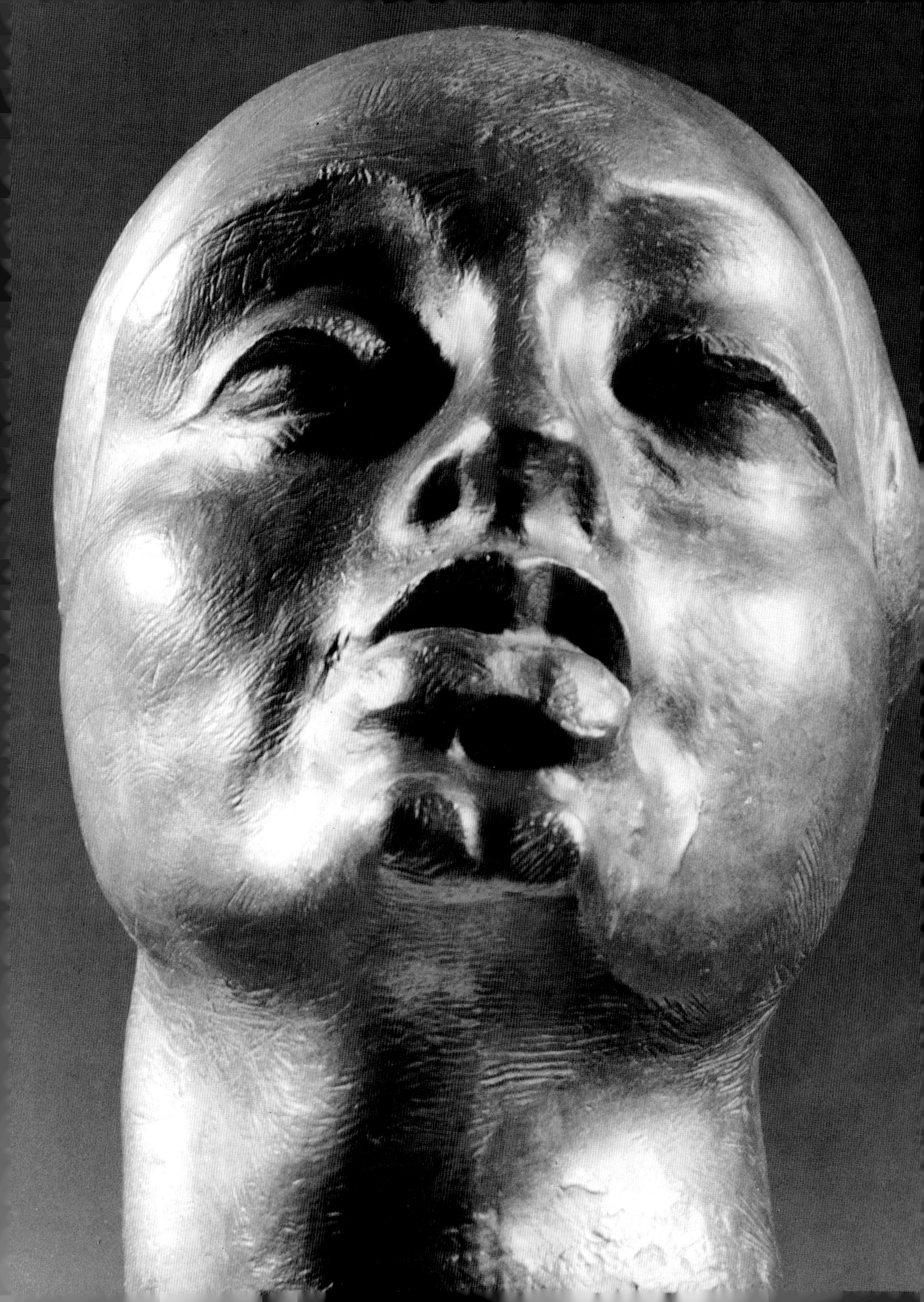

"To some people his nudes have seemed laden with grossness, though anyone who looks can see that their flesh is not debased, but as buoyant as a Gupta sculpture or the frescoes at Ajanta."

A. Hyatt Mayor

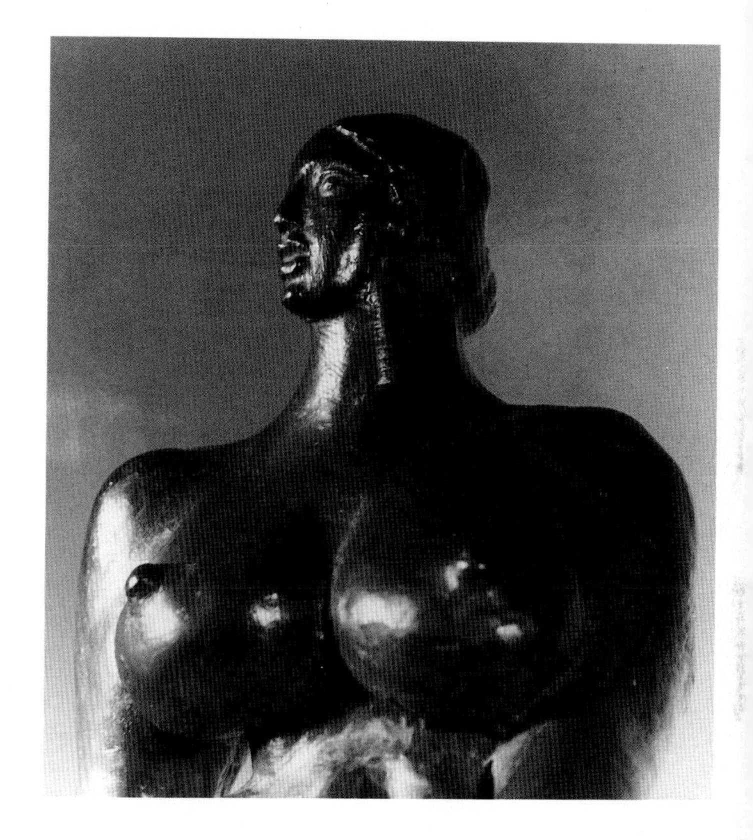

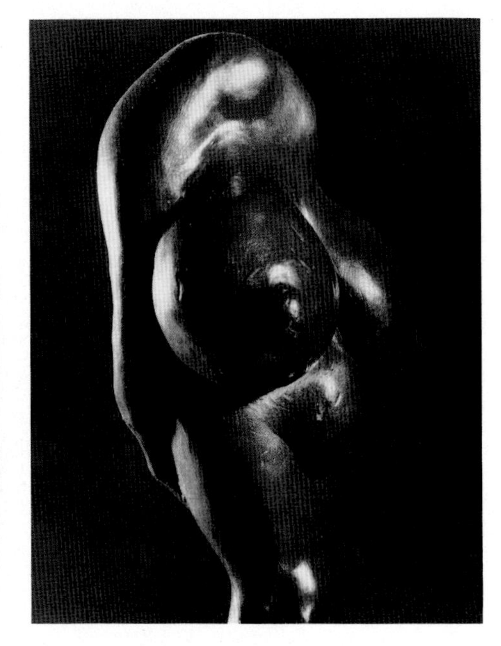

 TORSO *1928*

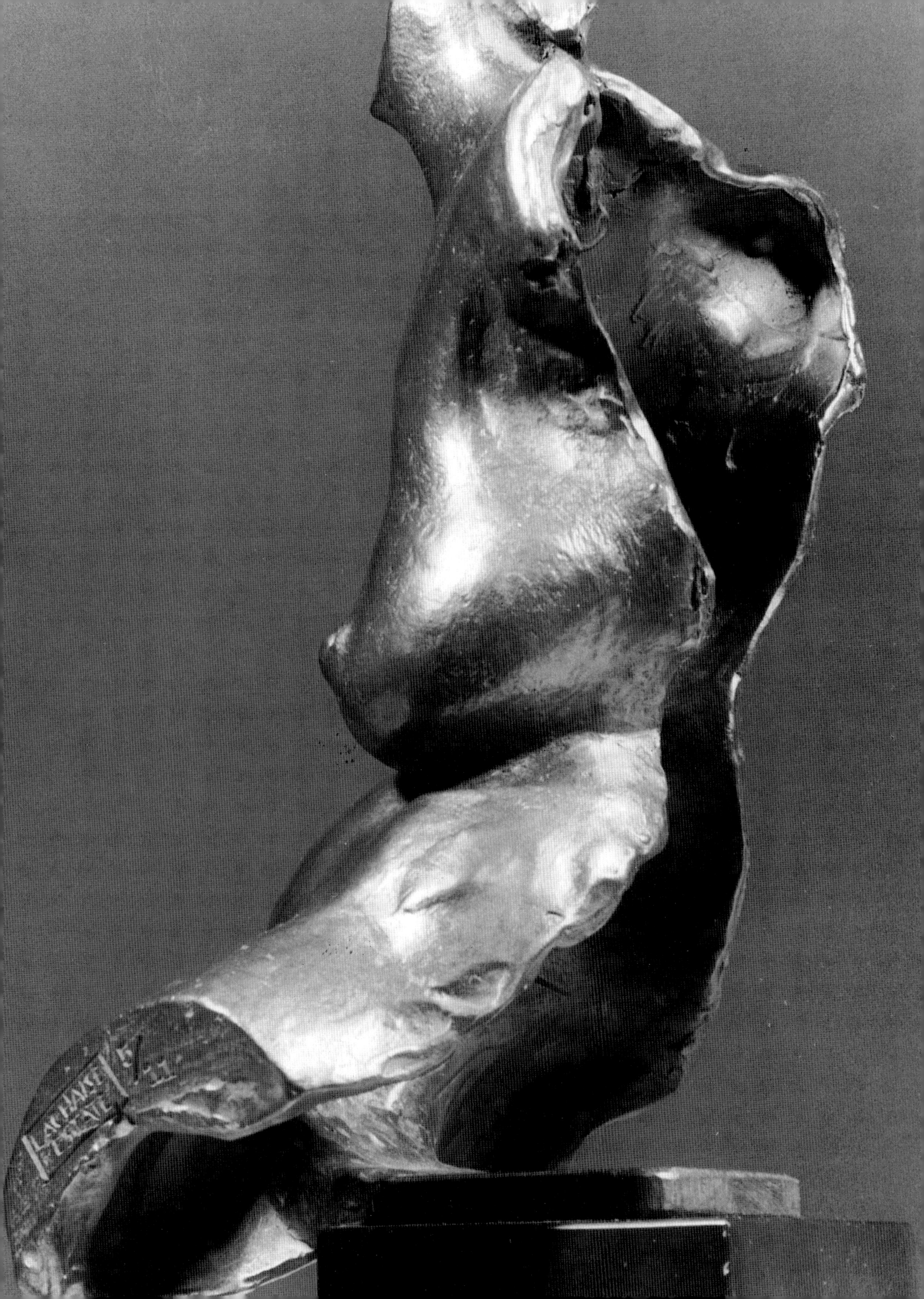
LACHAISE

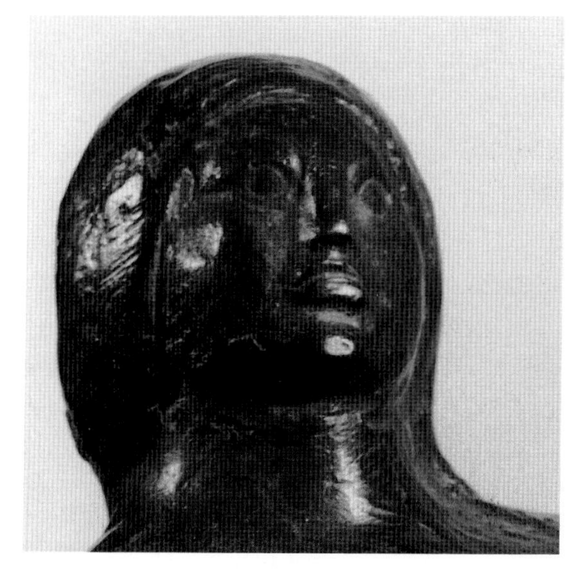

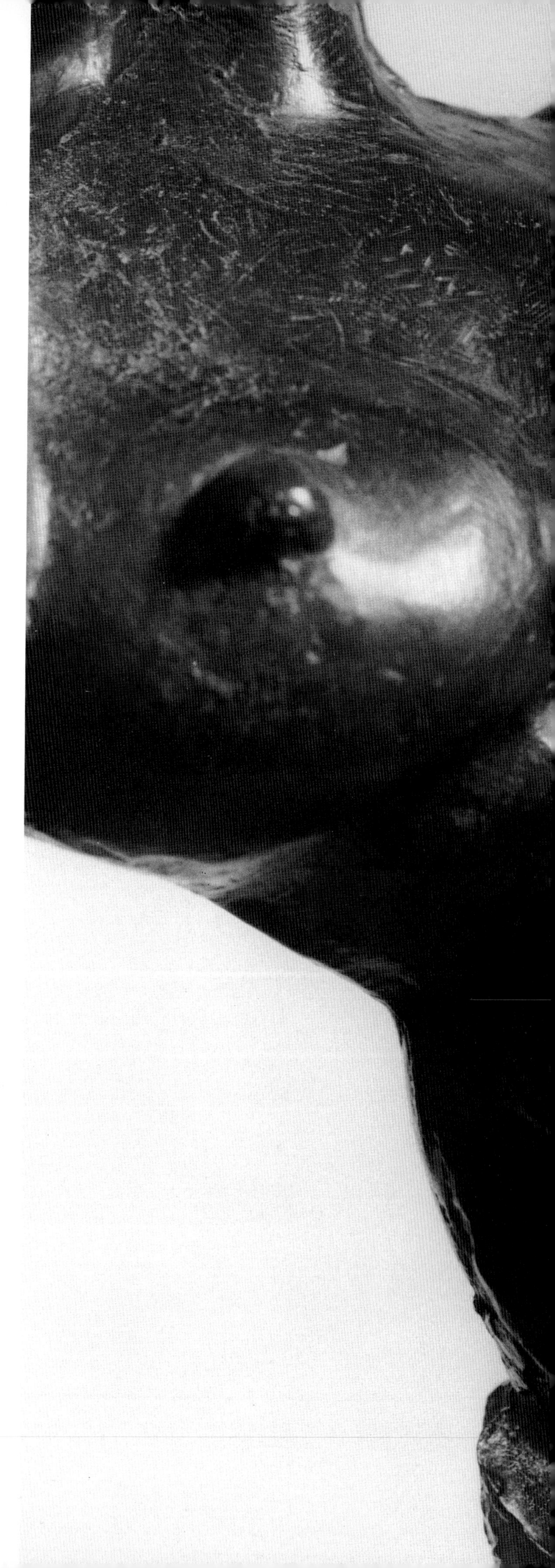

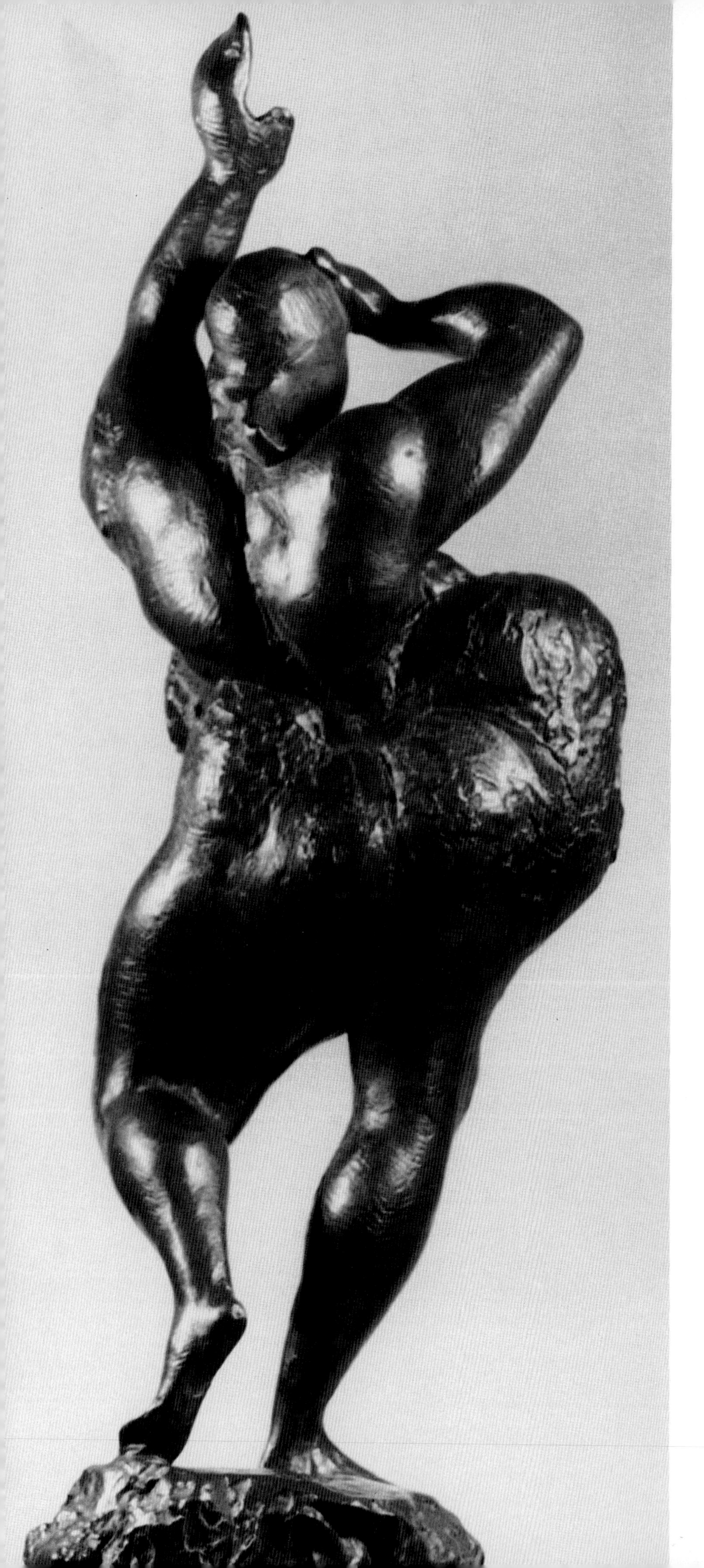

BURLESQUE FIGURE *1930*

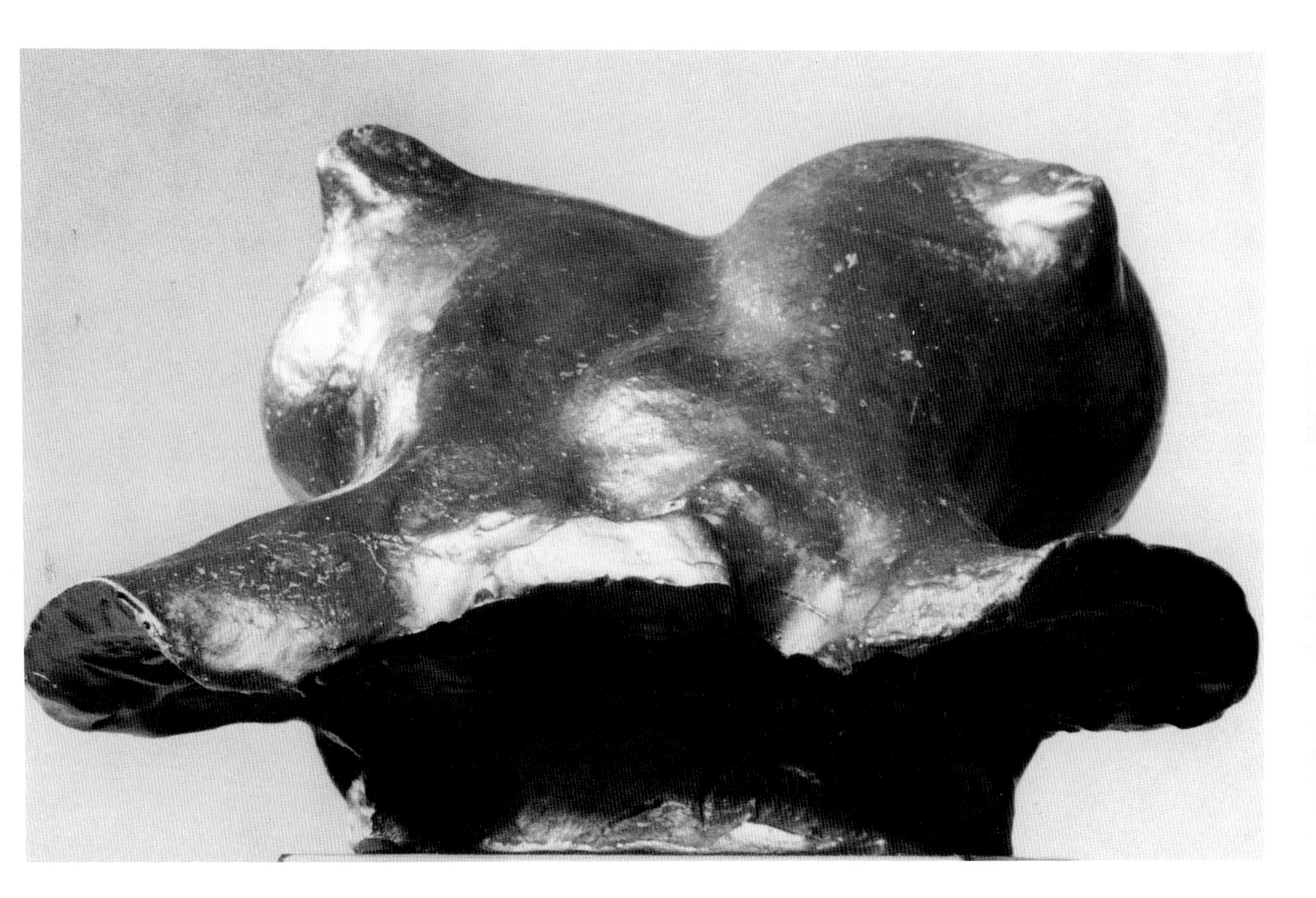

BREASTS, SMALL *1930*

SEATED WOMAN HOLDING BREASTS *1931*

TORSO
1930-1932

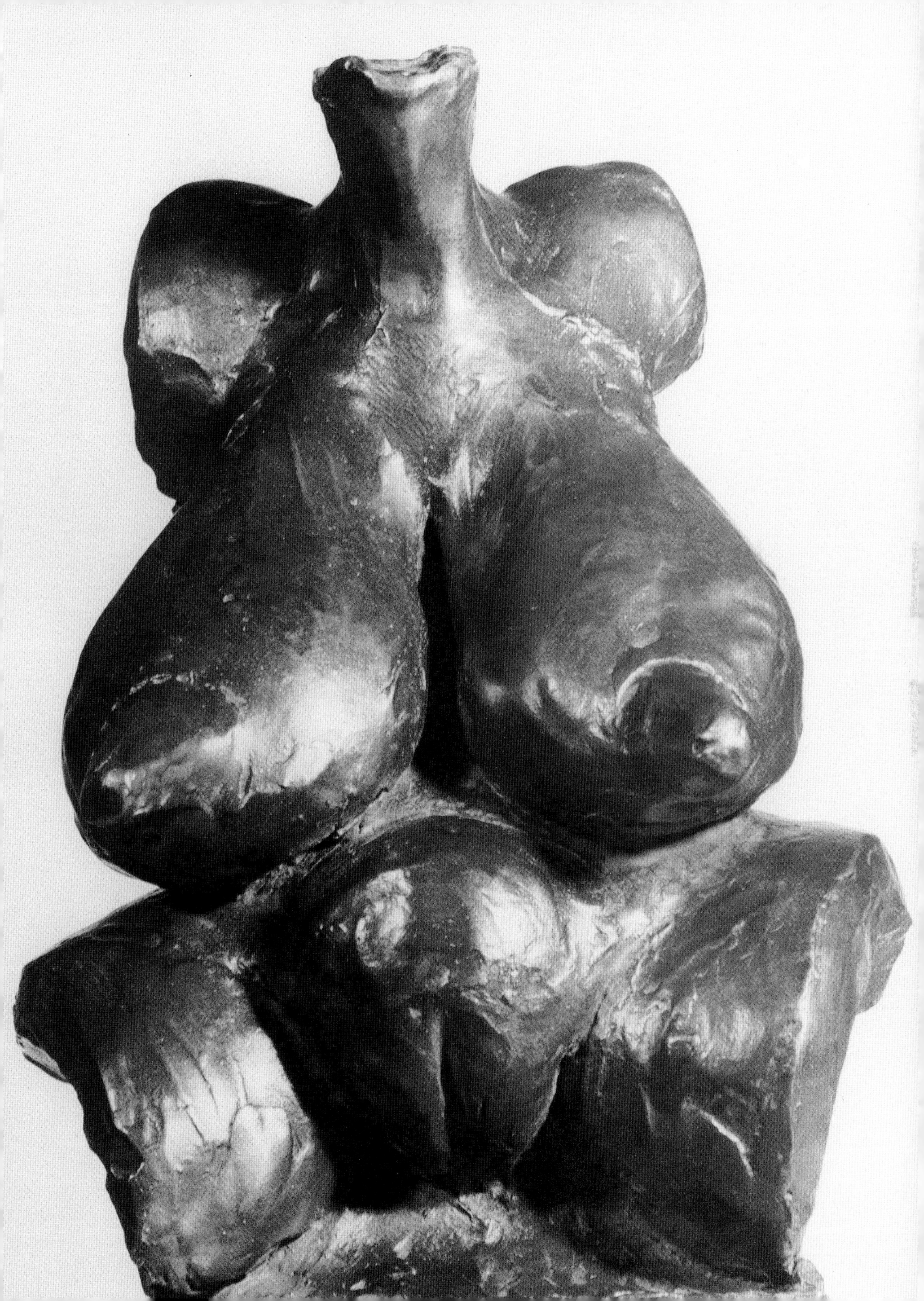

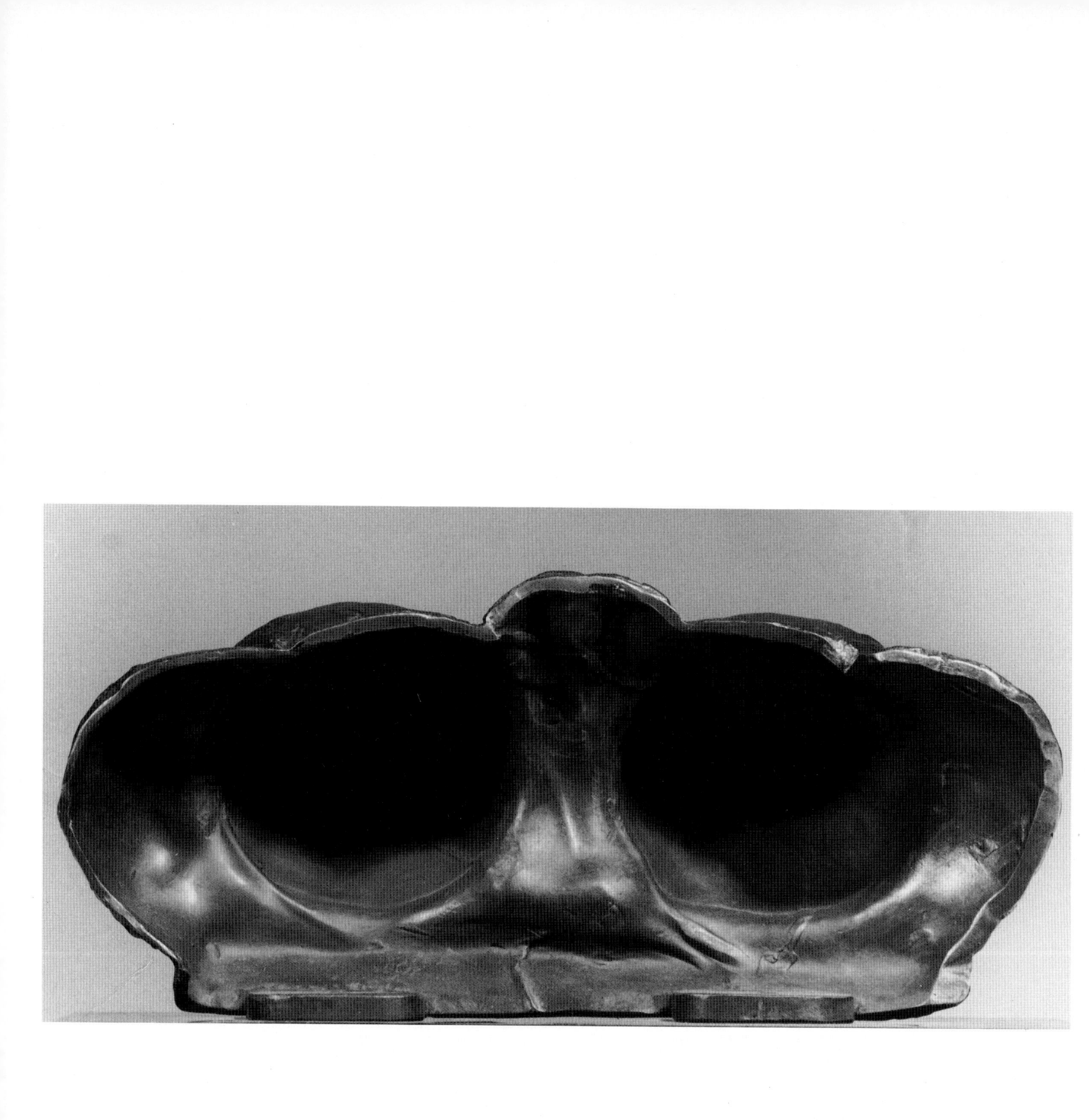

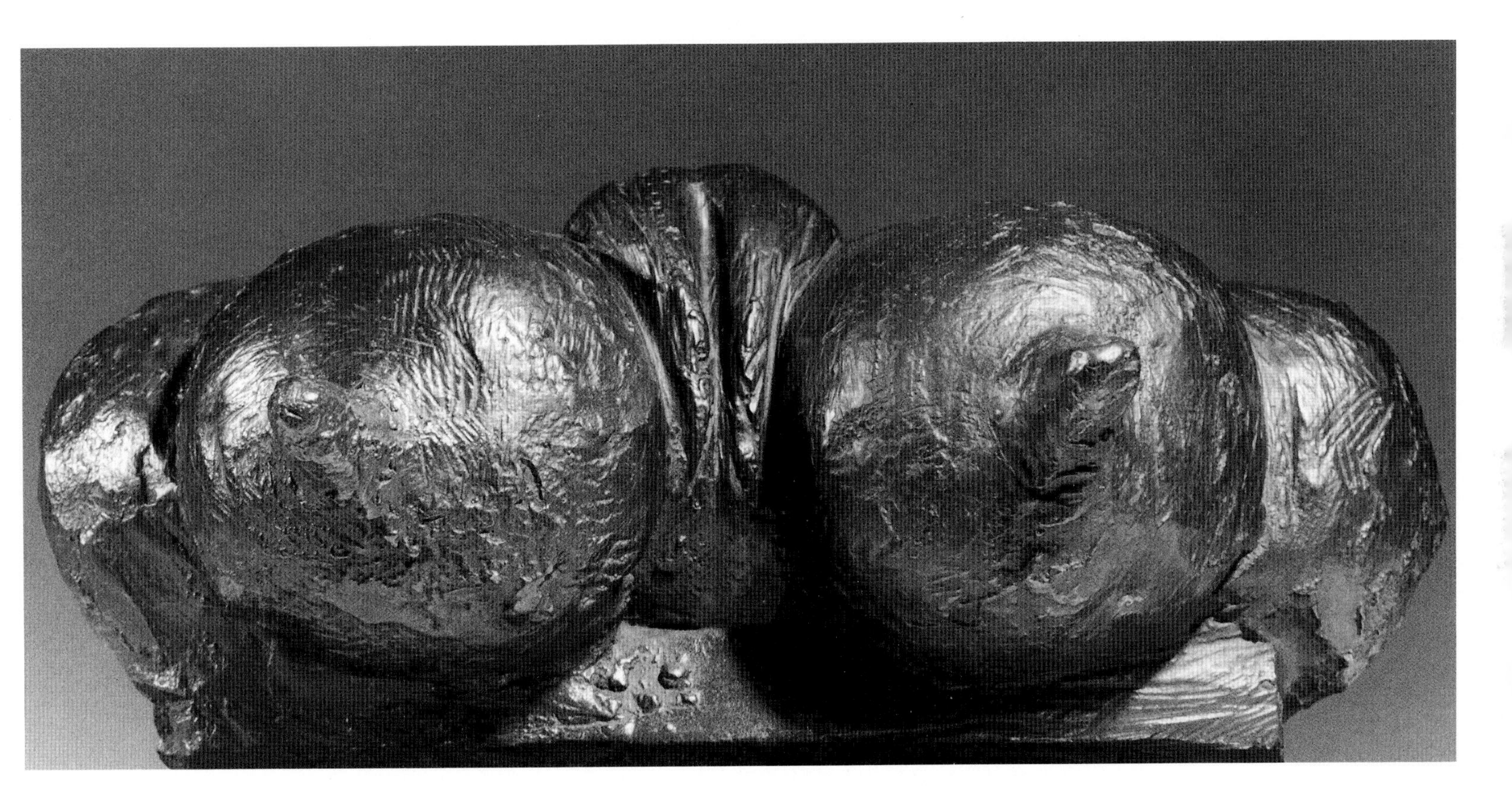

MAN WALKING (PORTRAIT OF LINCOLN KIRSTEIN) *1933*

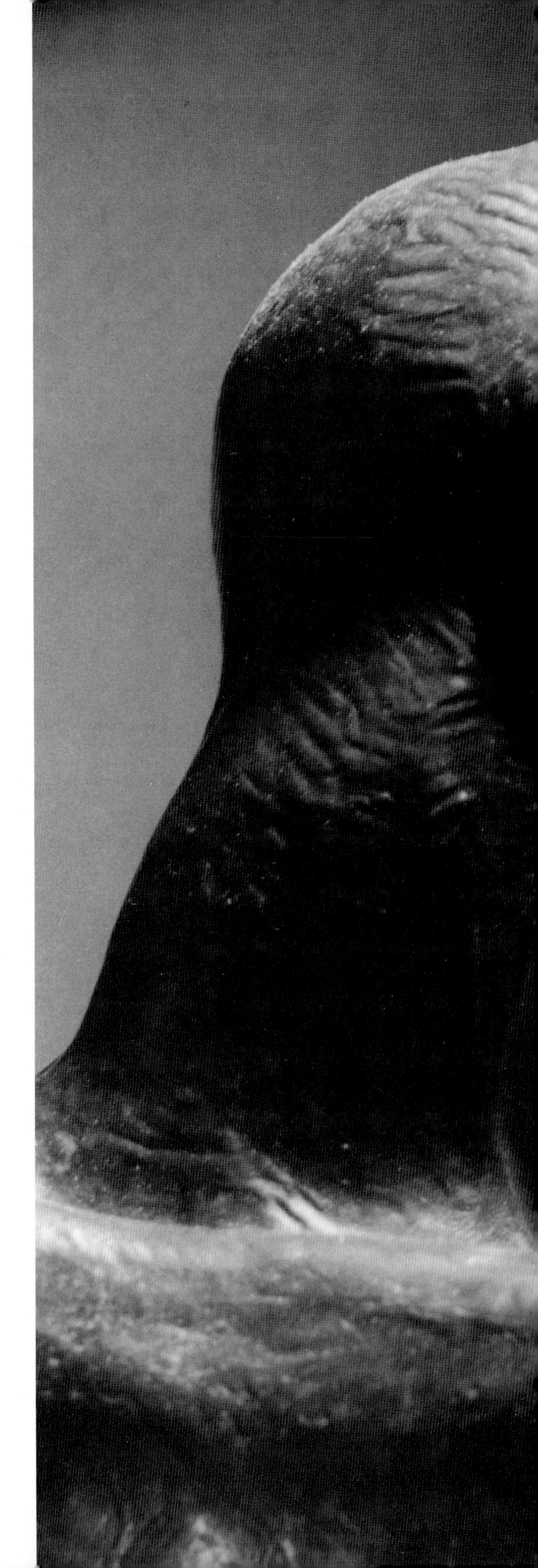

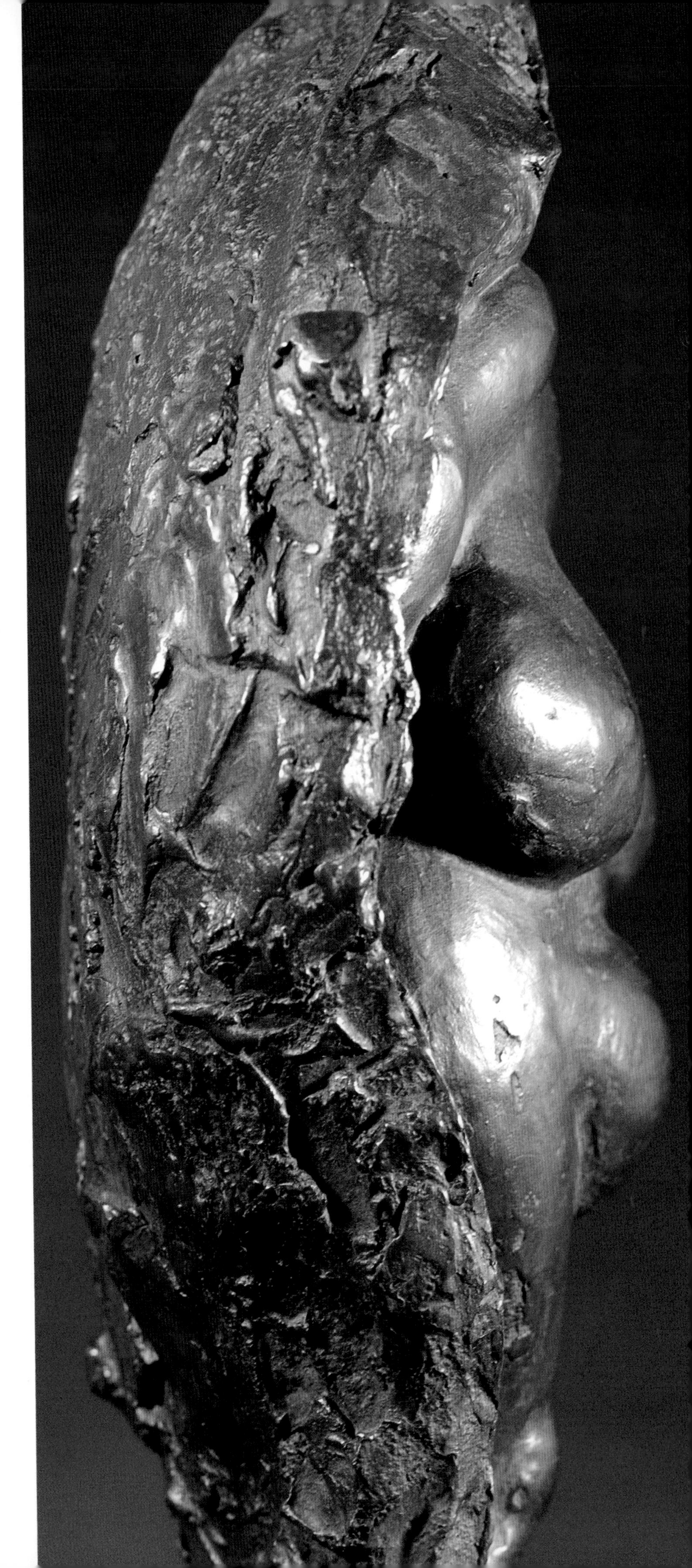

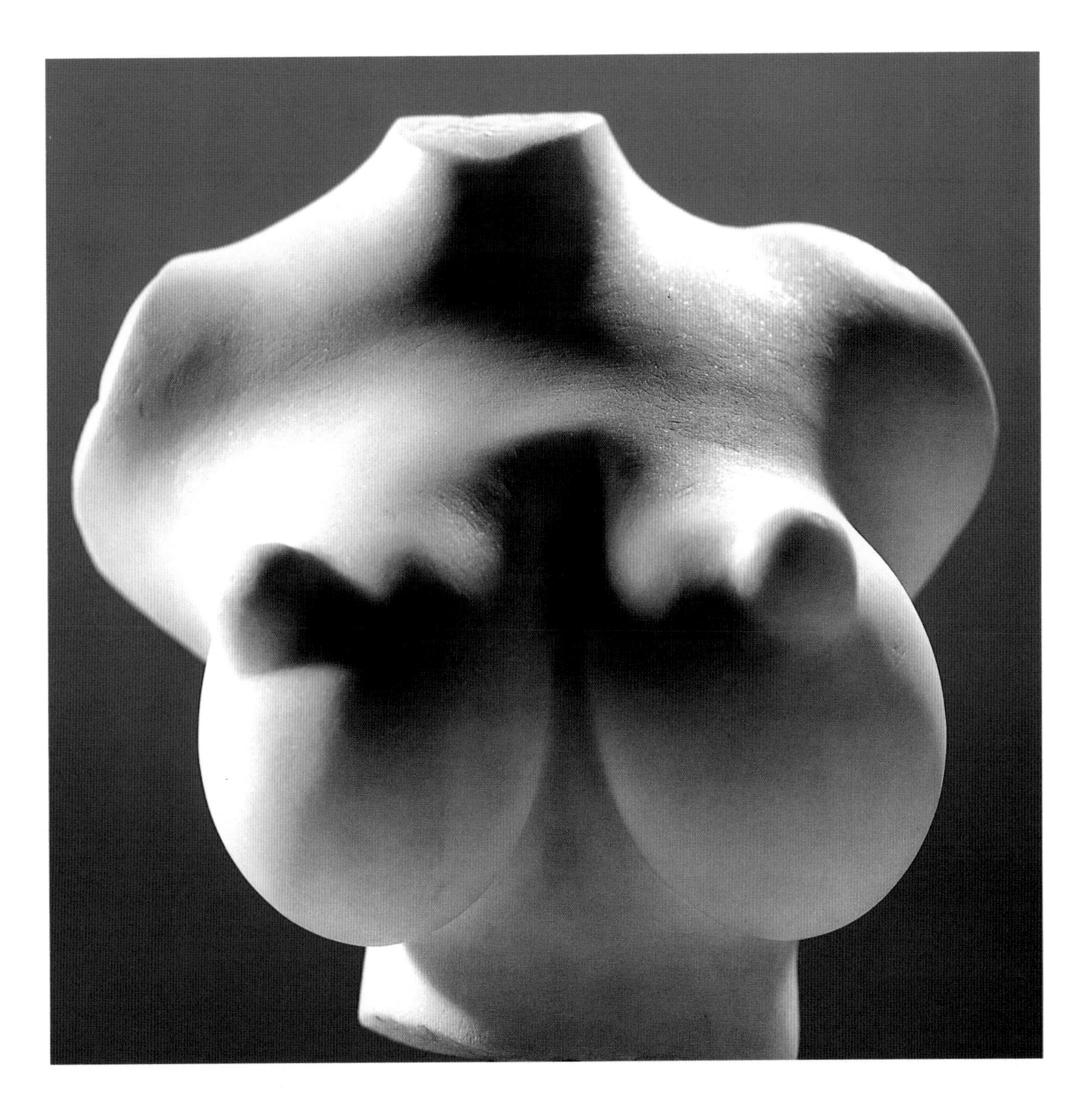

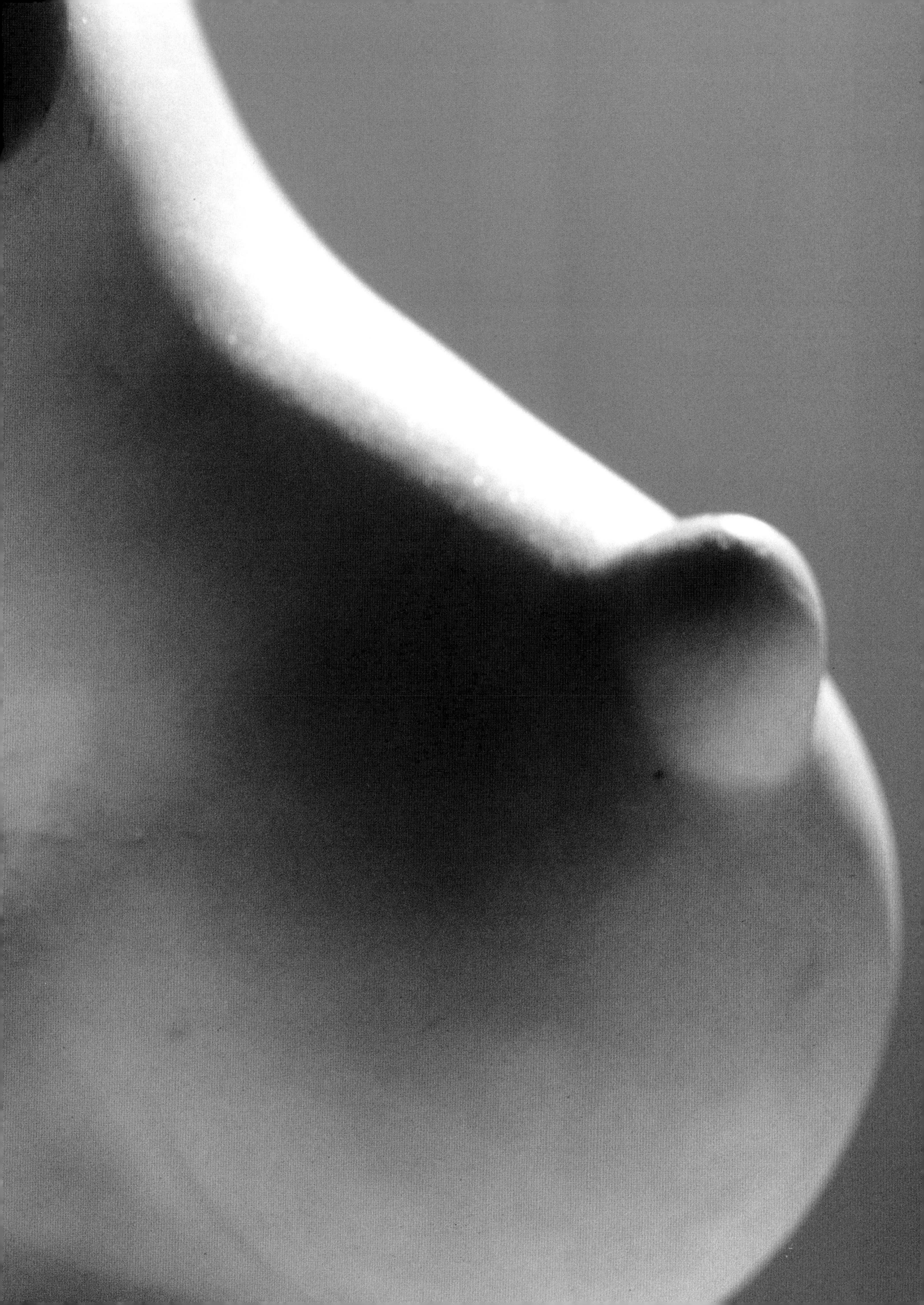

"Lachaise did not work from nature because he had a powerful vision that has haunted men since time immemorial of a voluptuous mother goddess who is neither madonna nor whore, but an abundant, generous, fertility and creation symbol."

Barbara Rose

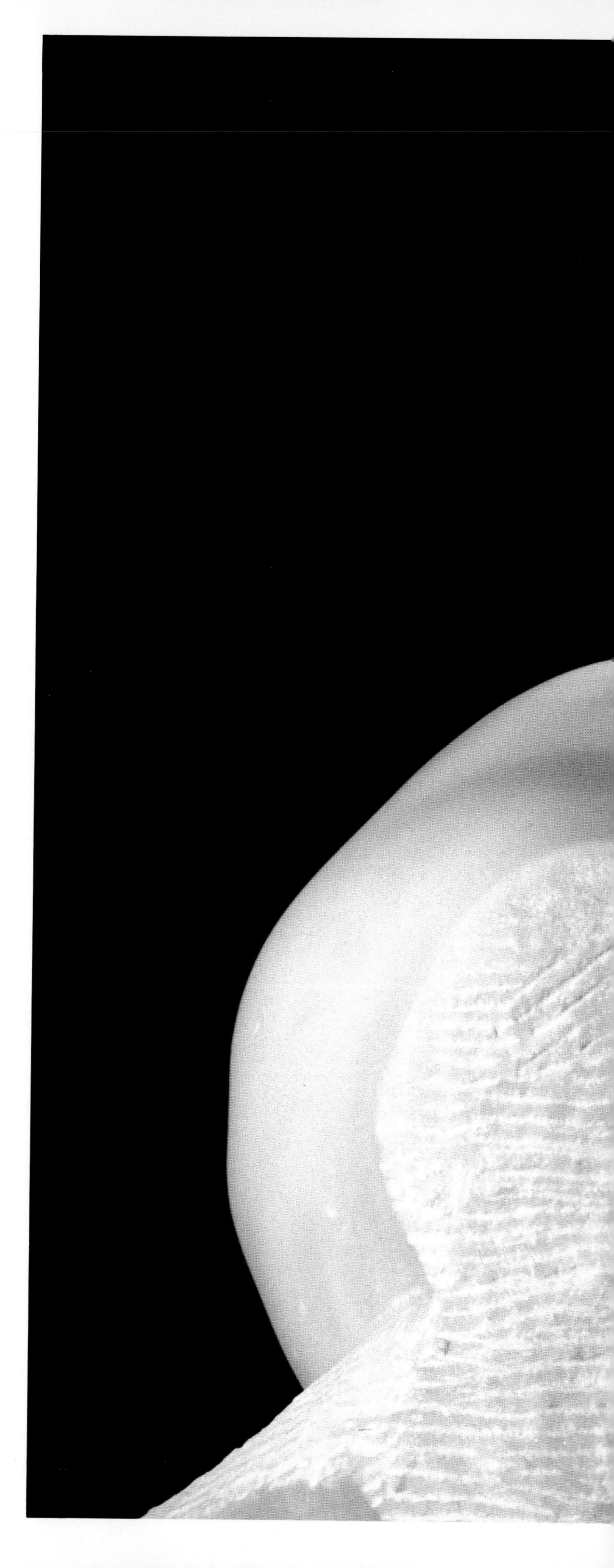

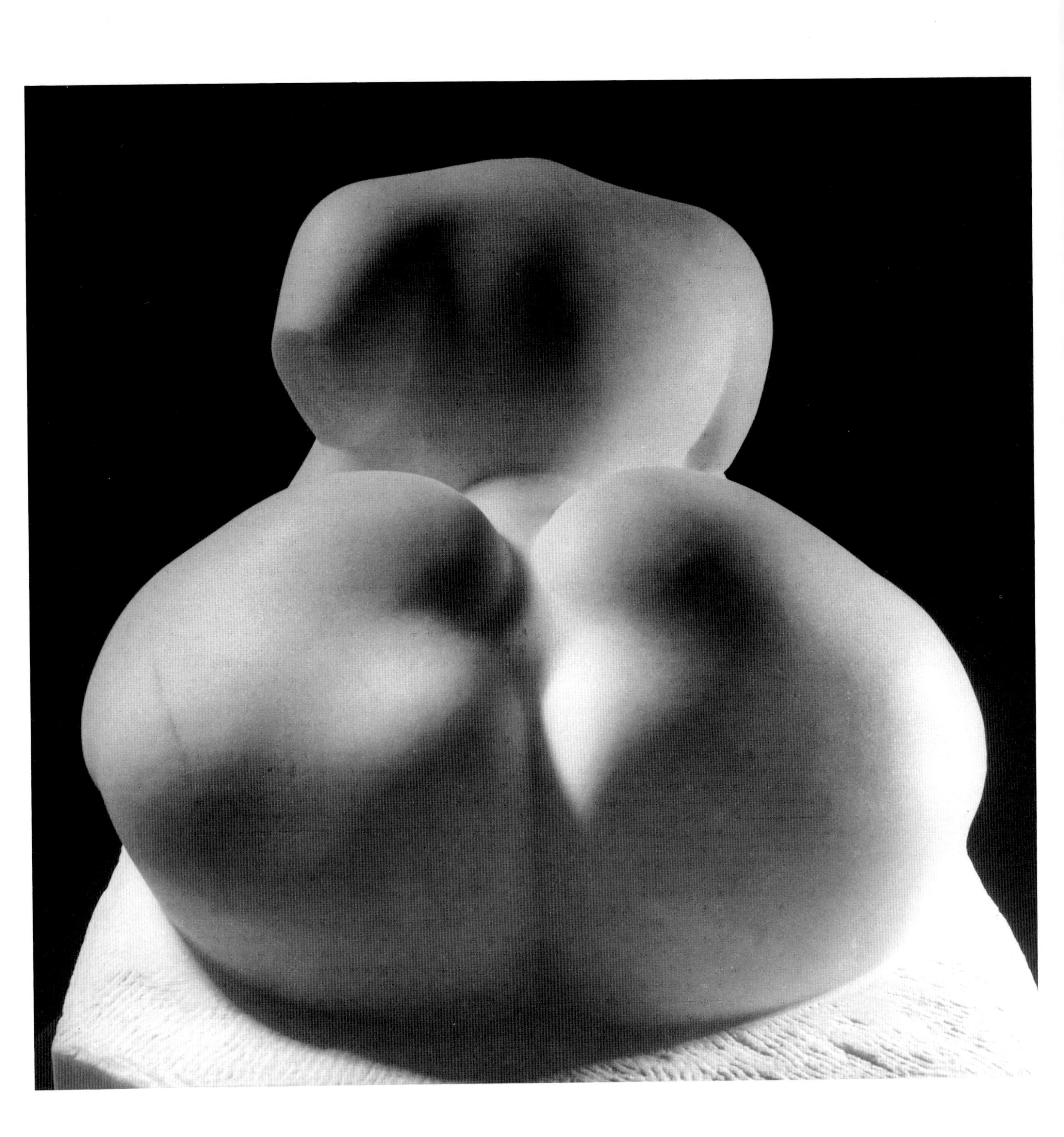

KNEES *1933*

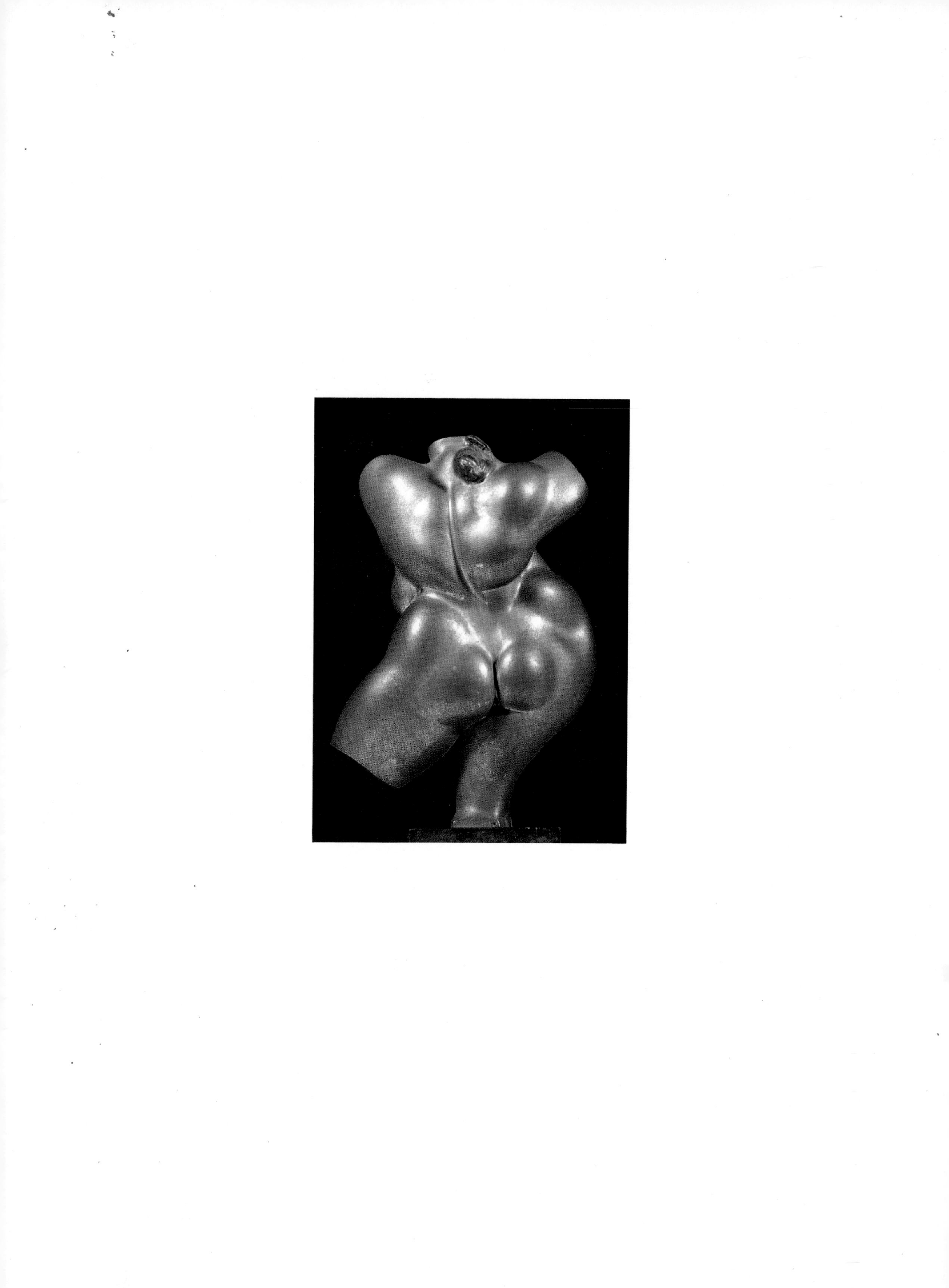

 FEMALE FIGURE (TORSO) *1931*

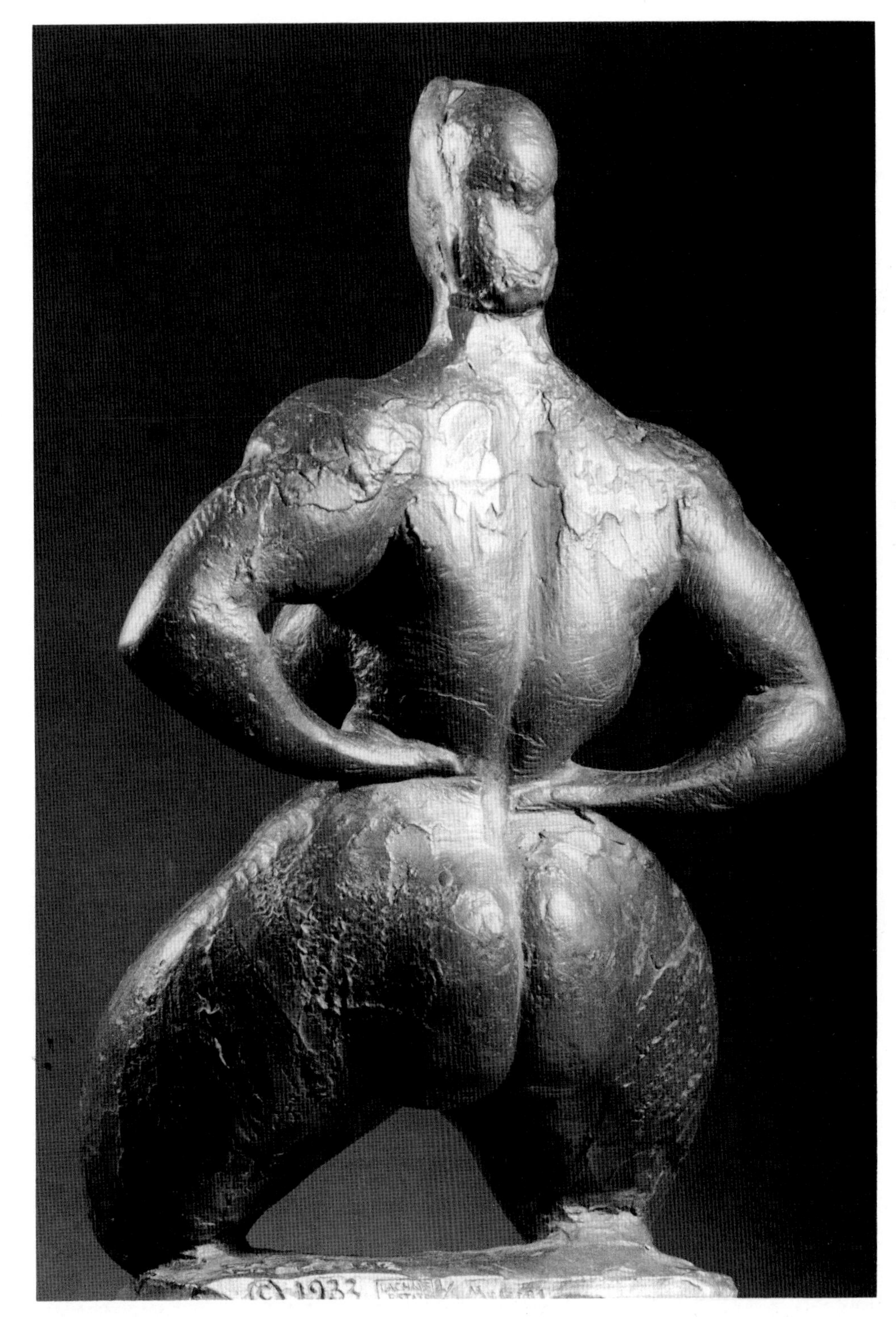

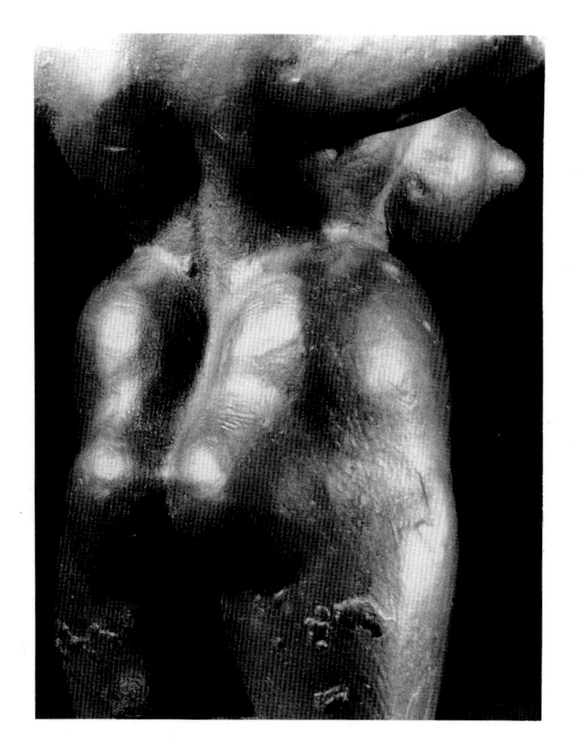

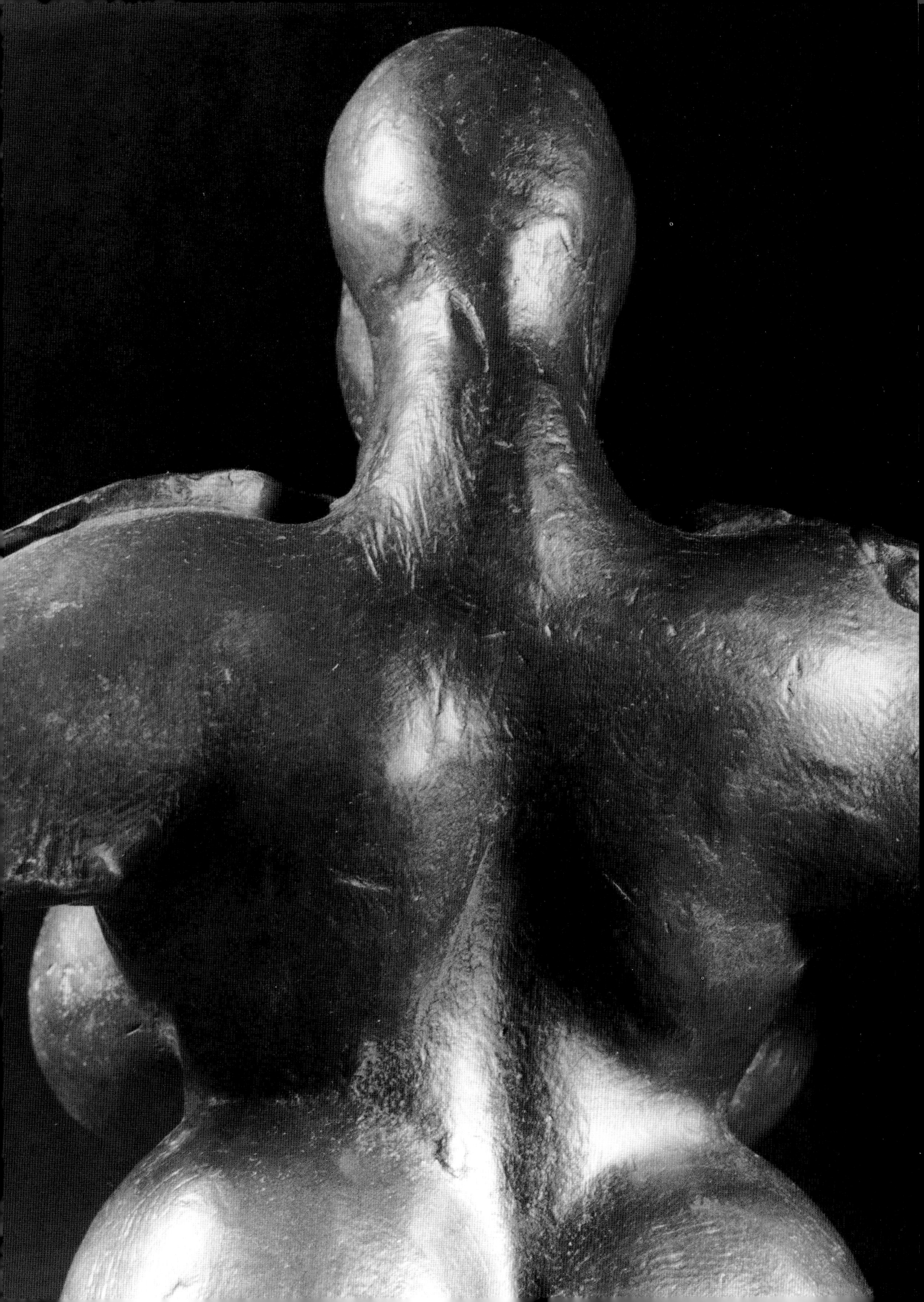

"Lachaise's increasing reduction of their essence to pendulous anatomical parts and finally to tumescent sex organs toward the end of his life, is not fetishistic but worshipful, a Western version of the Hindu yoni."

Barbara Rose

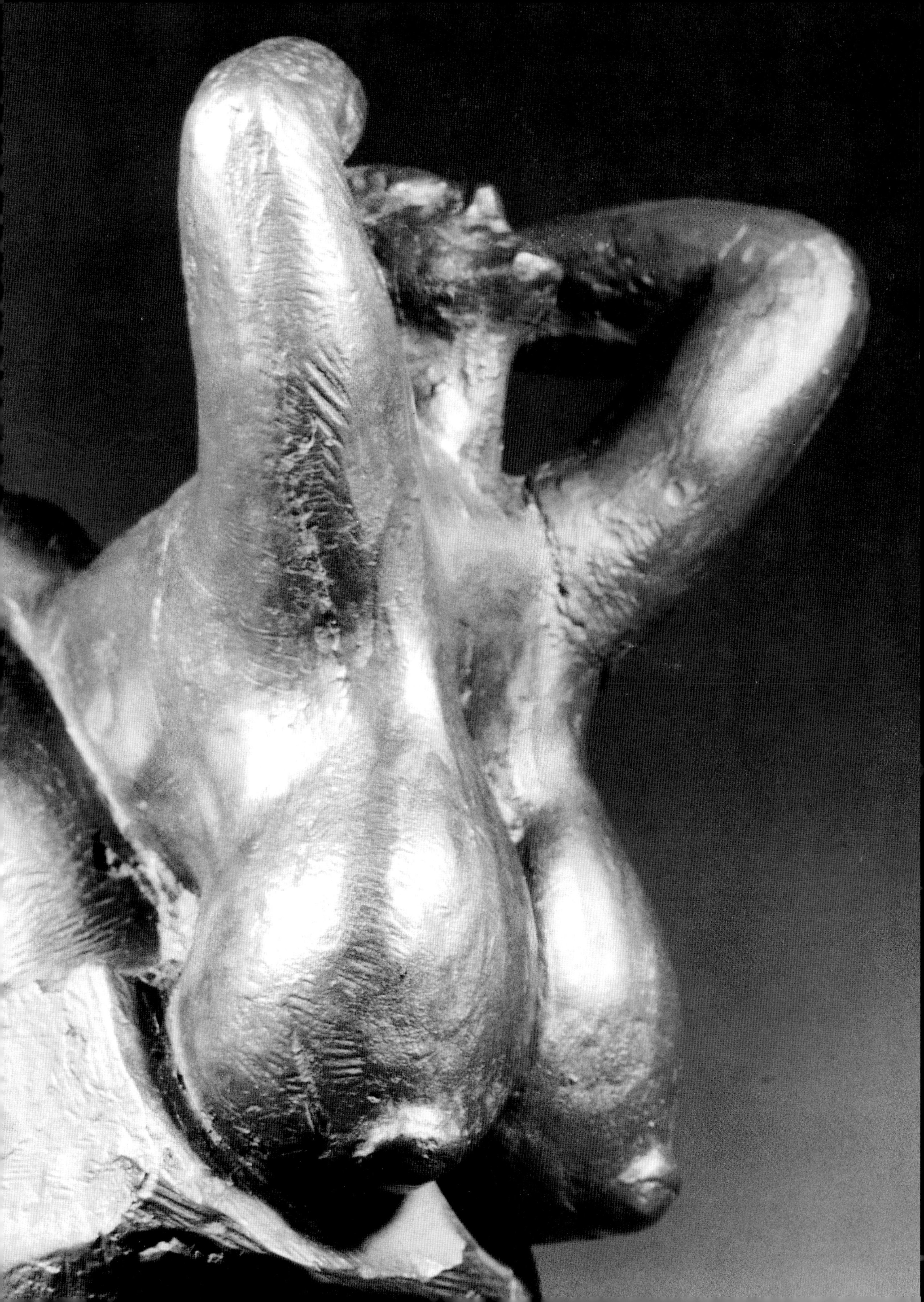

"No work is more gripping than *In Extremis*, where he depicts a kneeling woman whose enormous breasts are like sacks beside her hips and whose chin is thrust in the air. The work's blend of sexuality and violence recalls Giacometti's *Woman with Her Throat Cut*. But the violence does not come across as an assault on women, nor do Lachaise's exaggerated forms strive for parody."

Michael Kimmelman

"All art is a confession."

Gaston Lachaise

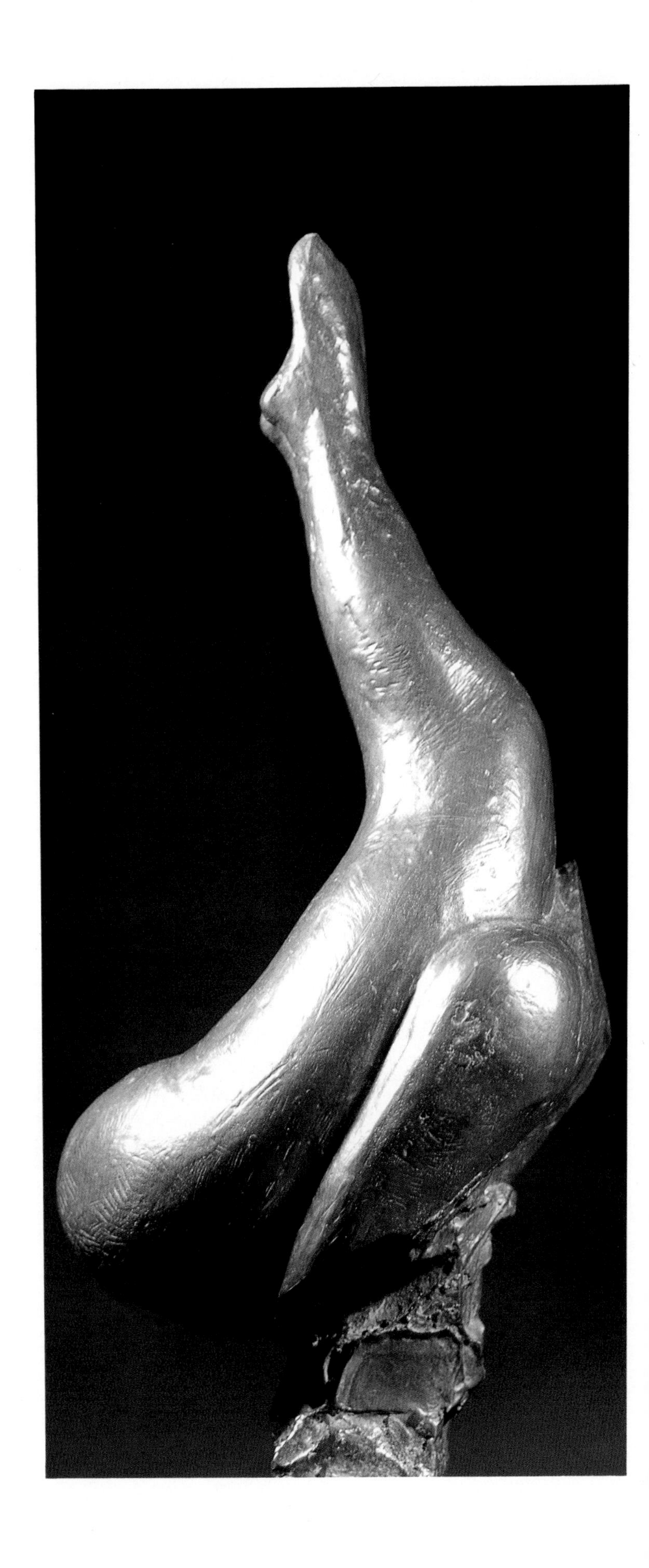

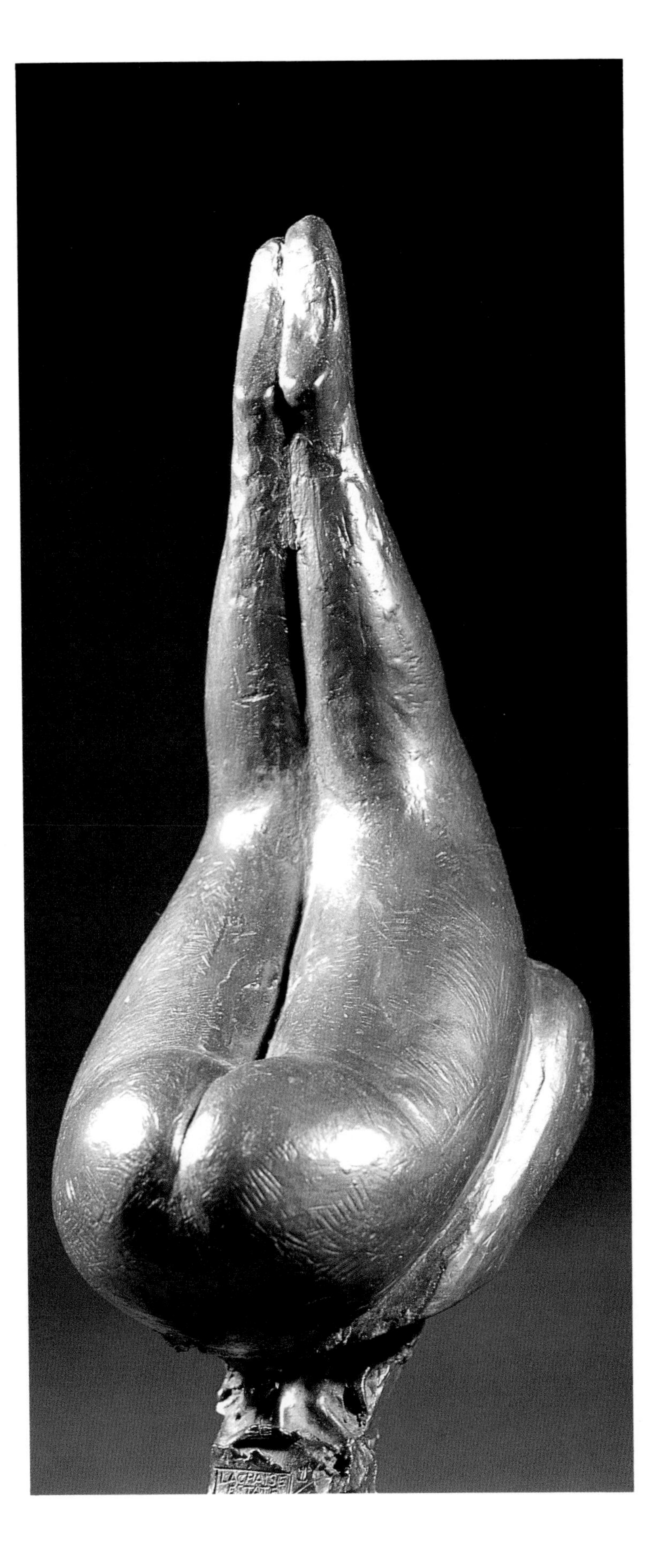

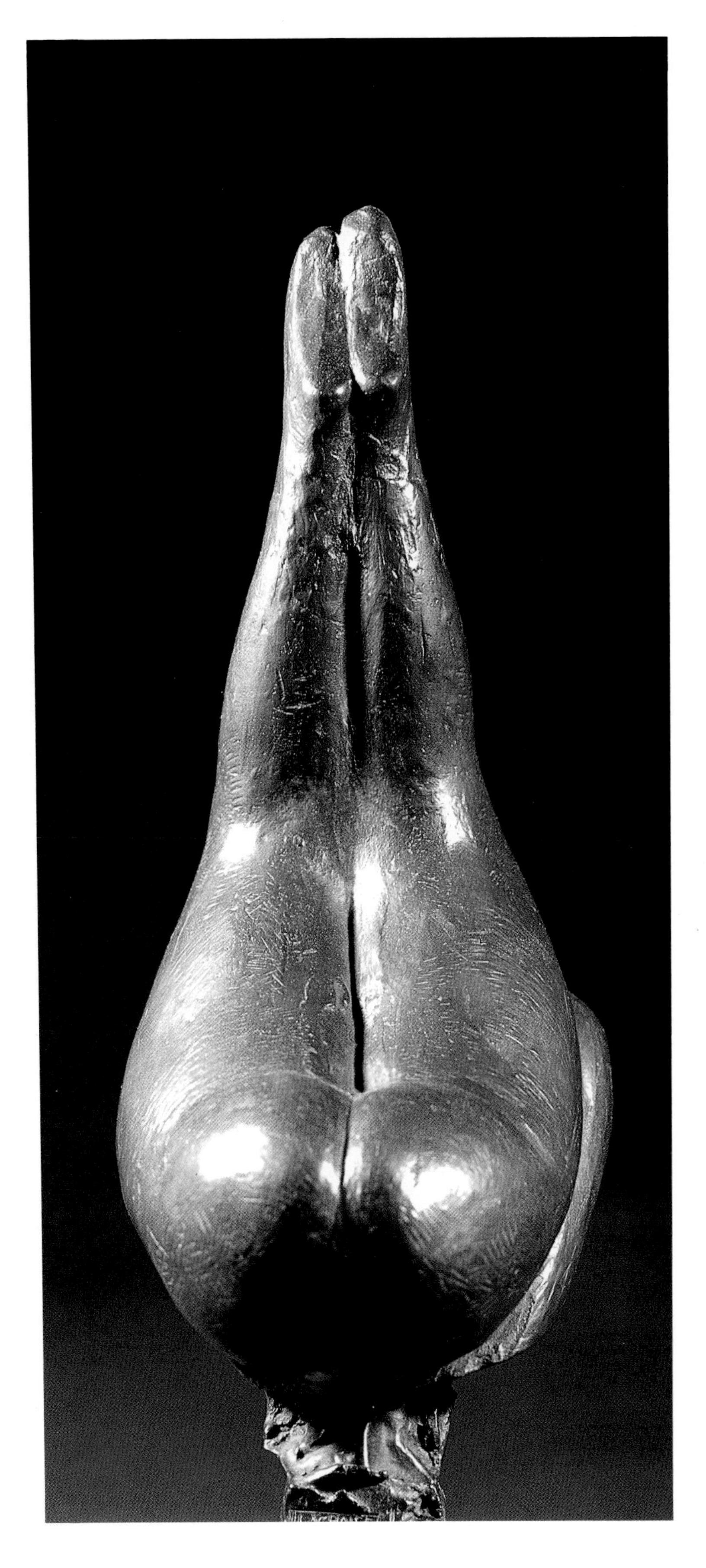

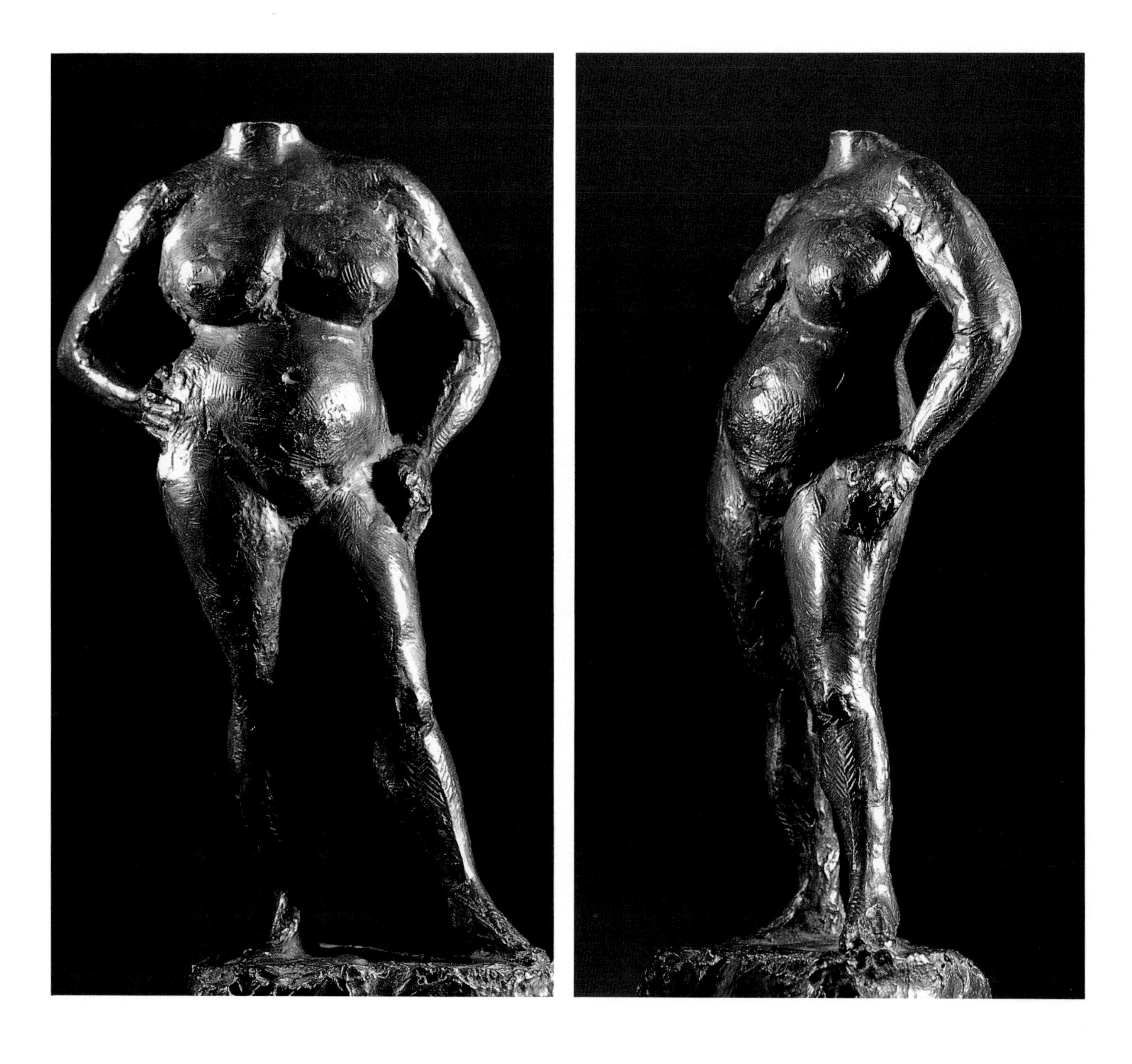

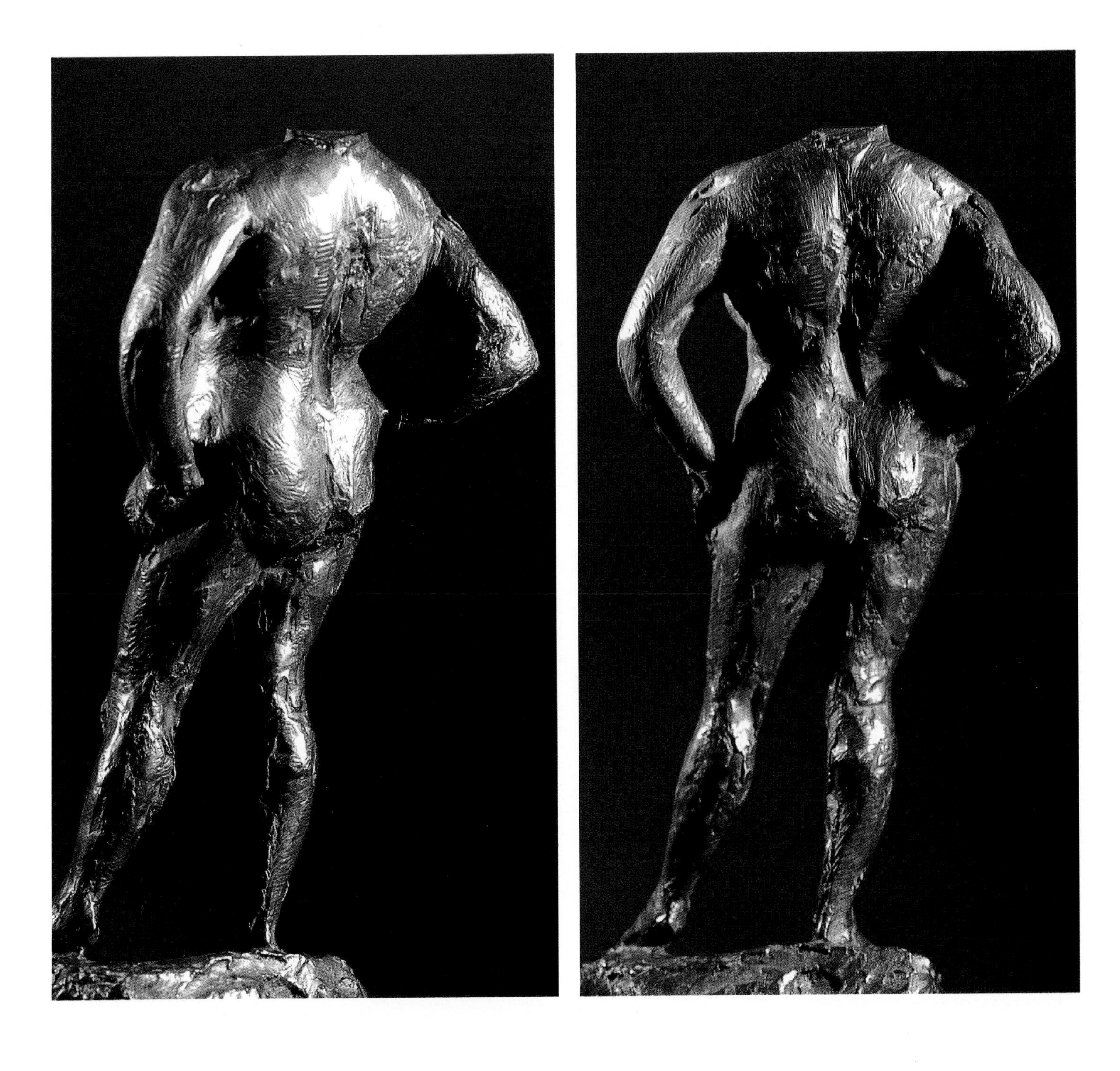

"He reached for passion, bereavement, tenderness, joy, the expression of sexual feeling, for the unknowable experiences of birth and even of death. His was a pantheistic expression of the artist's mission, not only having to do with art but with human life and experience, with mind and body, nature itself, perhaps only subconsciously recognized but converging in a single meaning beyond the intellect."

Gerald Nordland

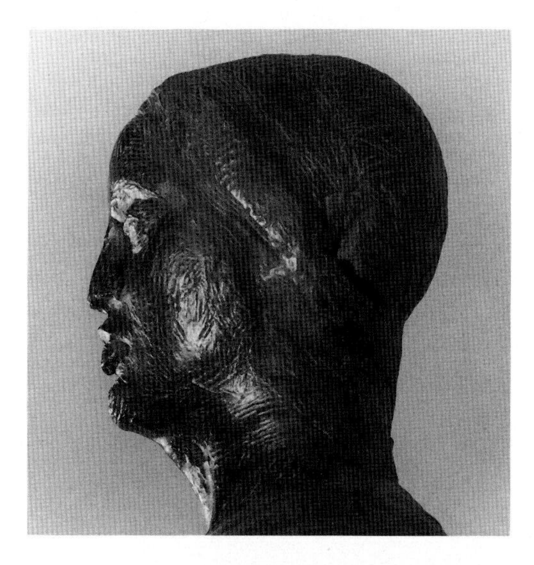

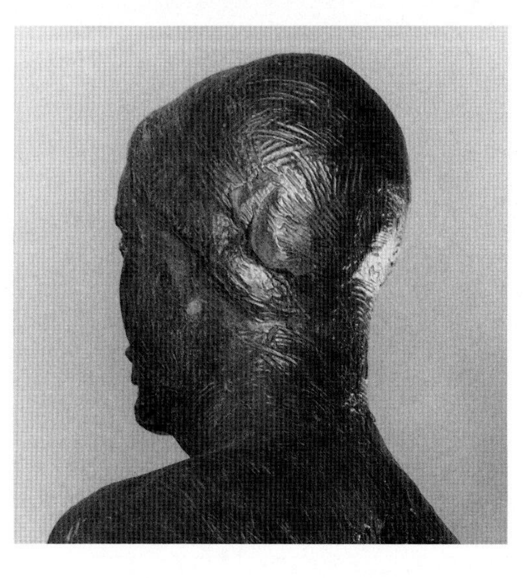

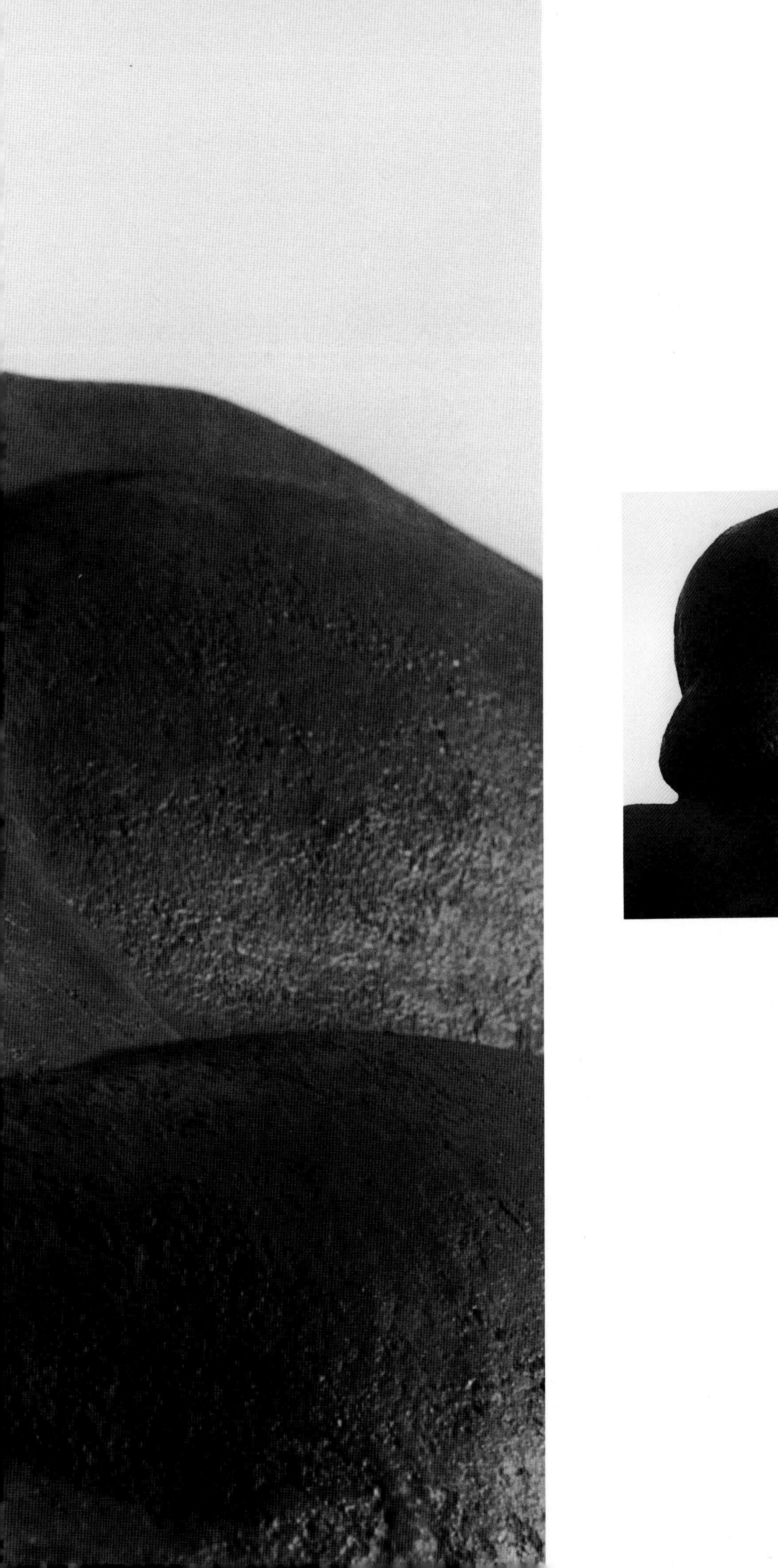

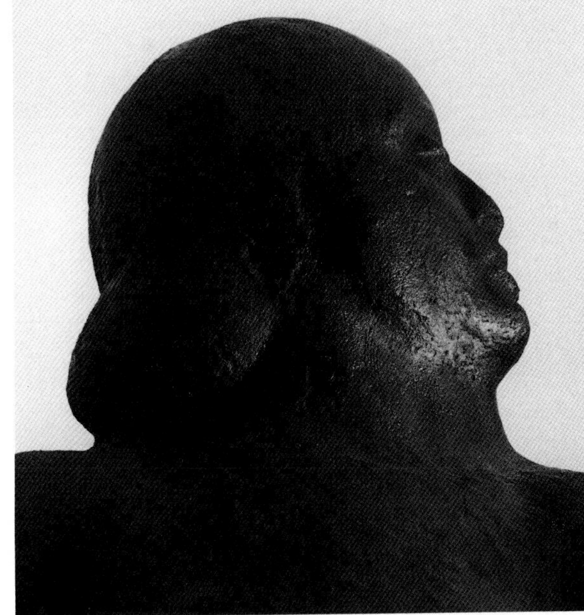

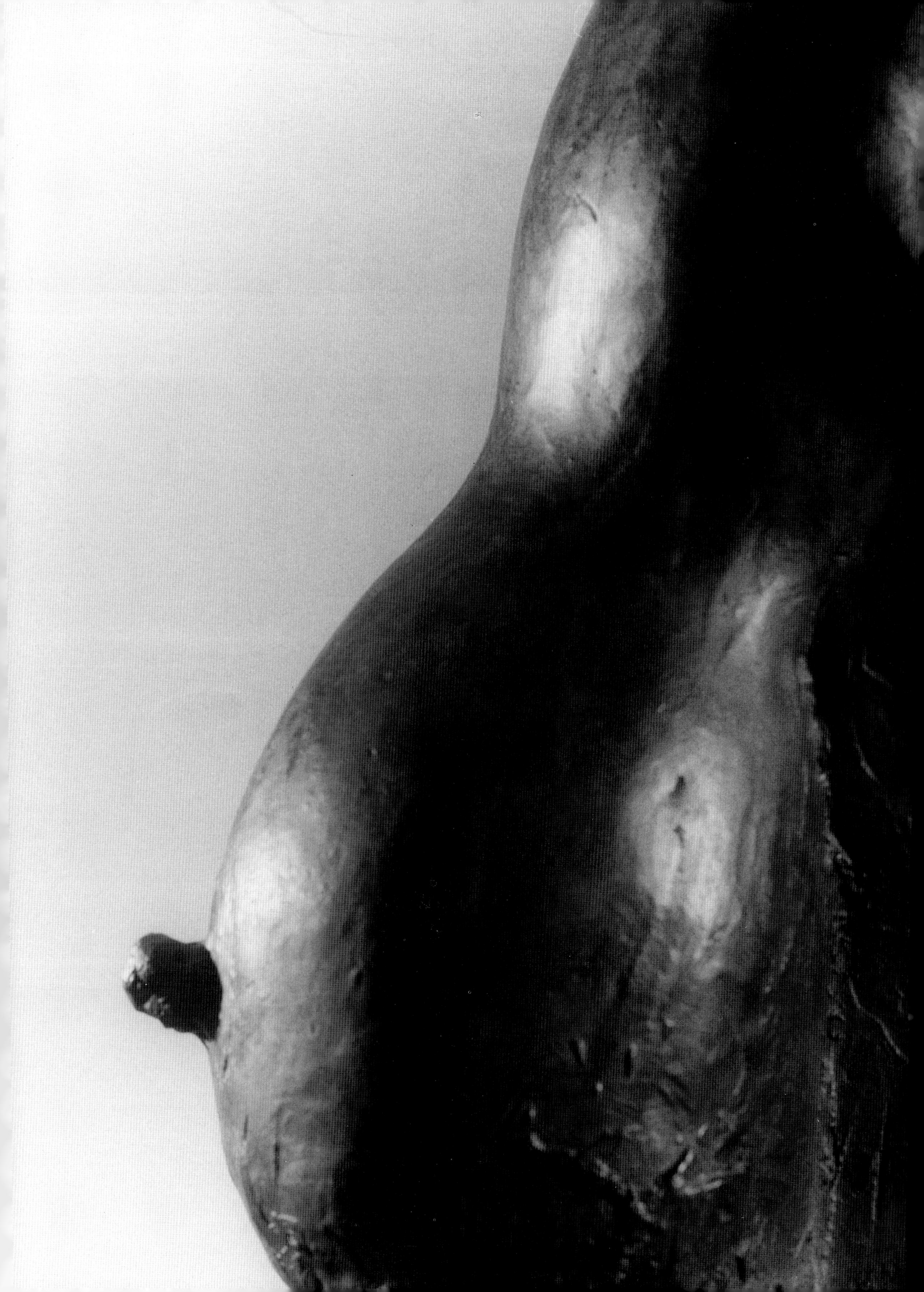

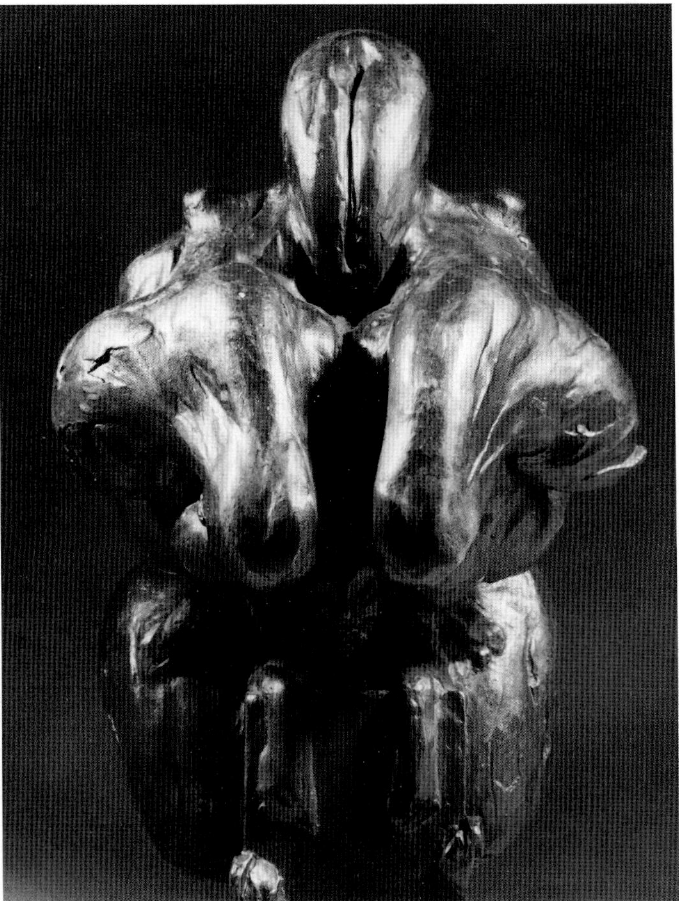

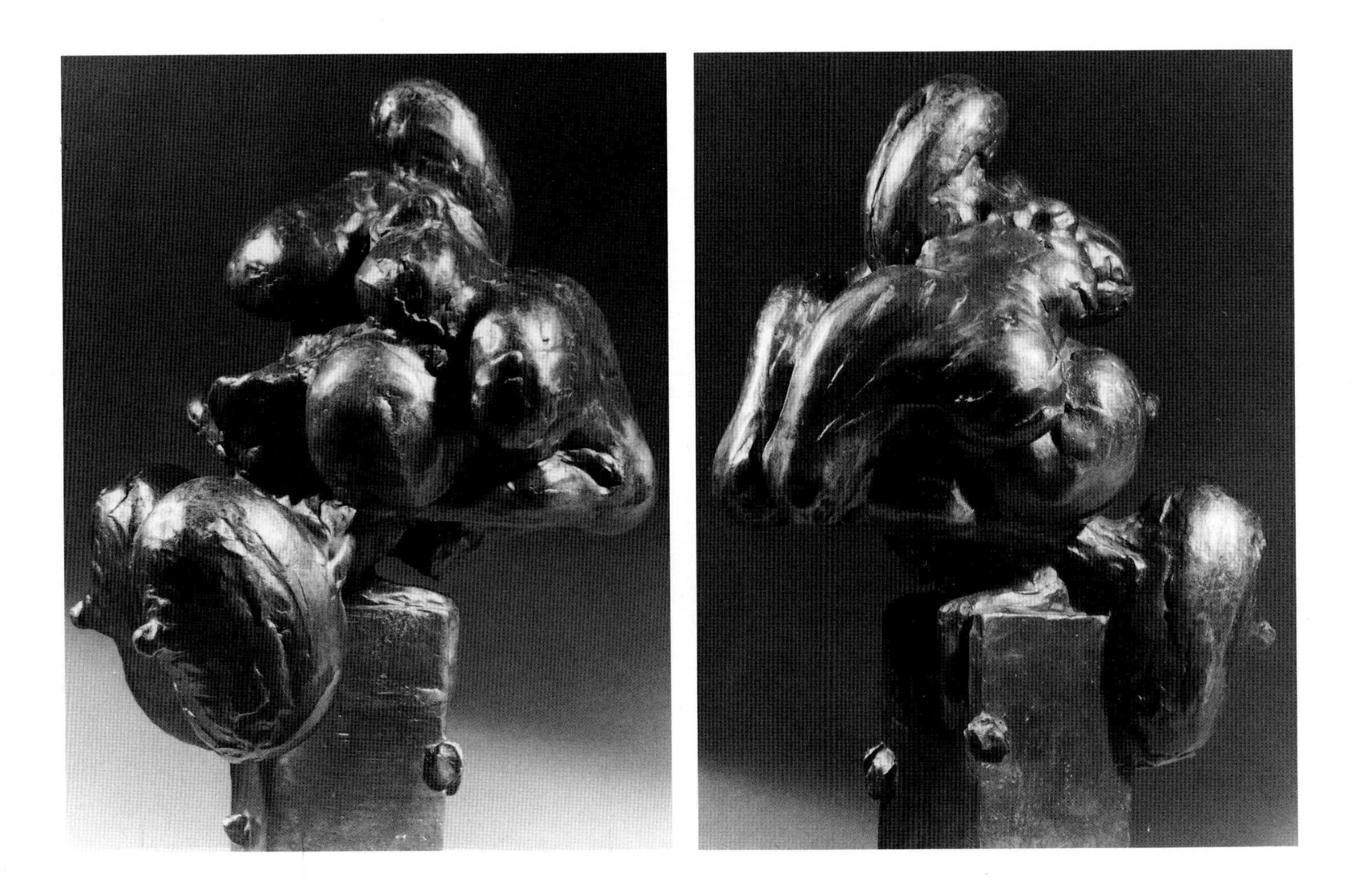

MADAME LACHAISE IN AN ARMCHAIR
(A PORTRAIT OF THE ARTIST'S MOTHER)
1912

THE PORTRAITS

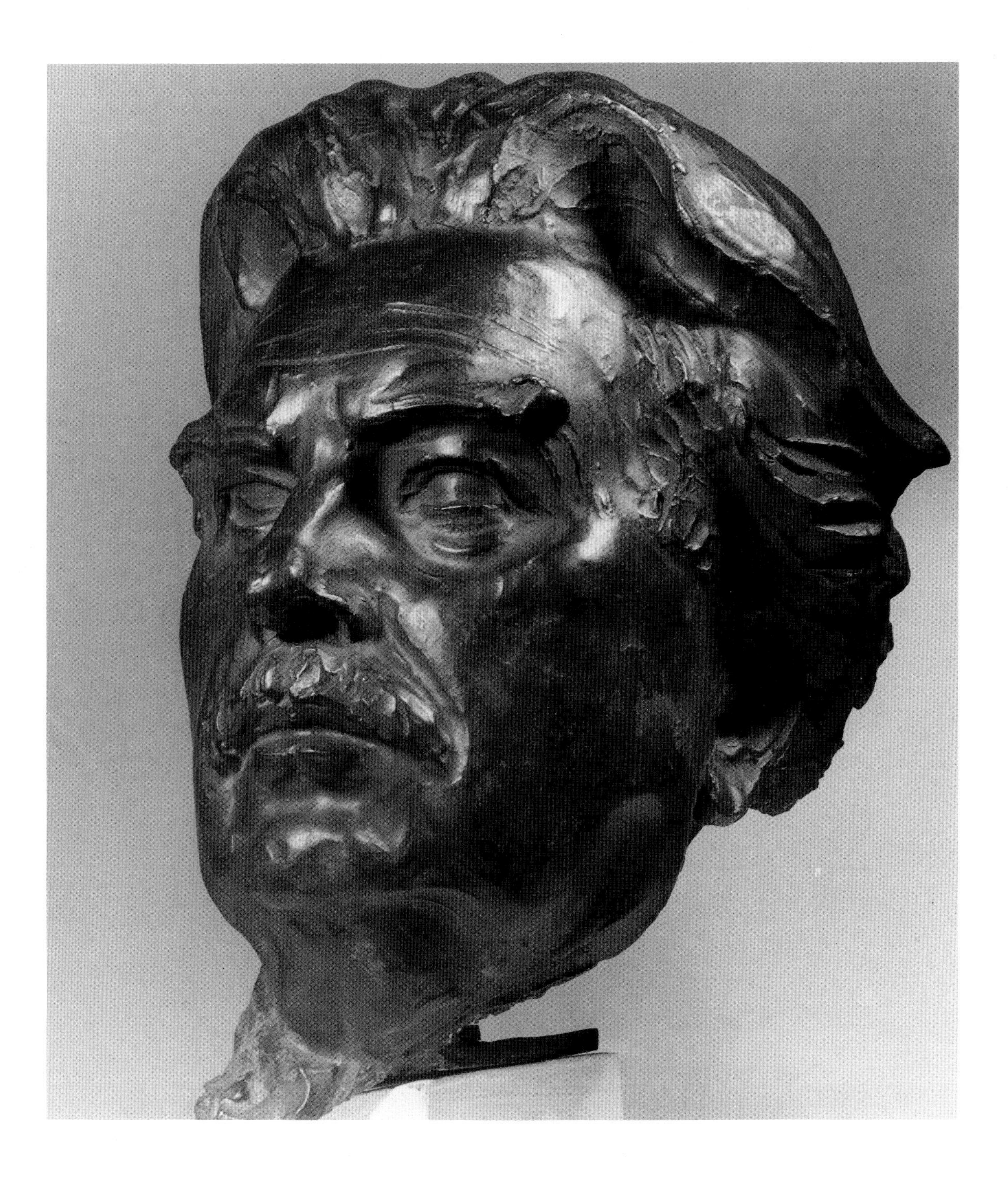

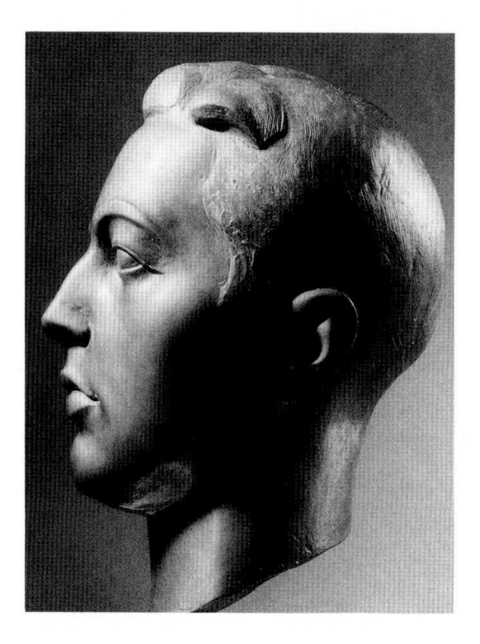

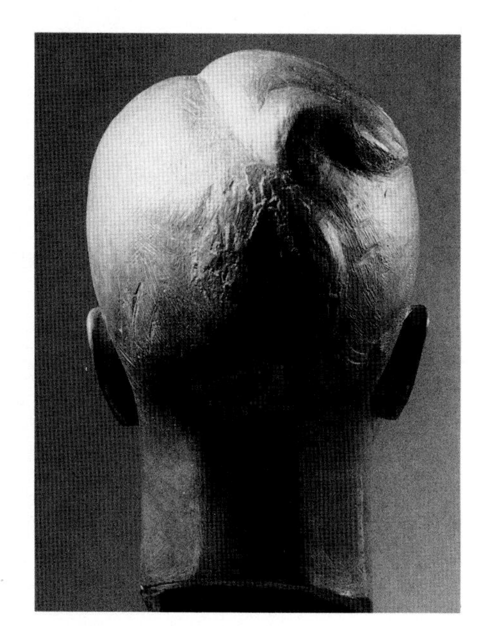

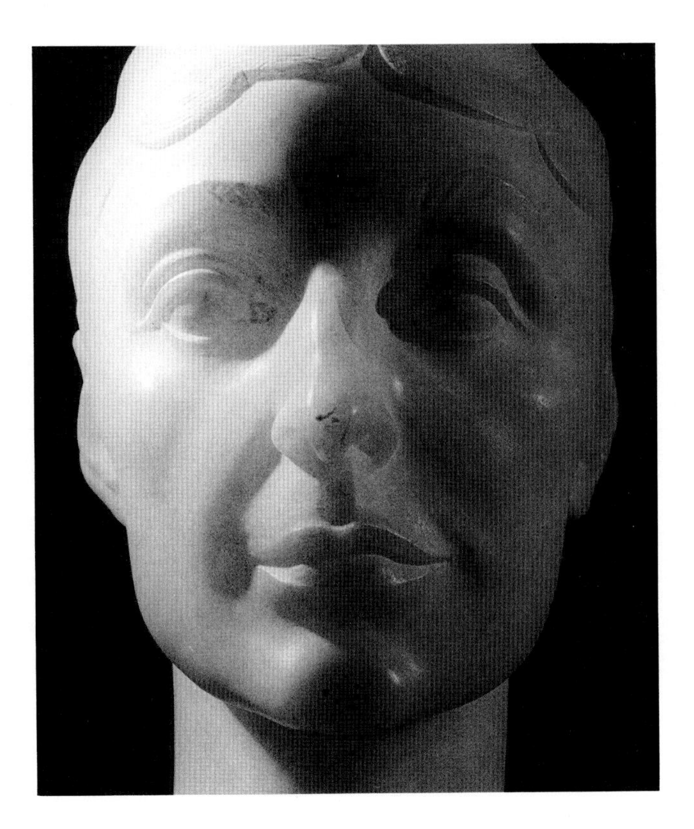

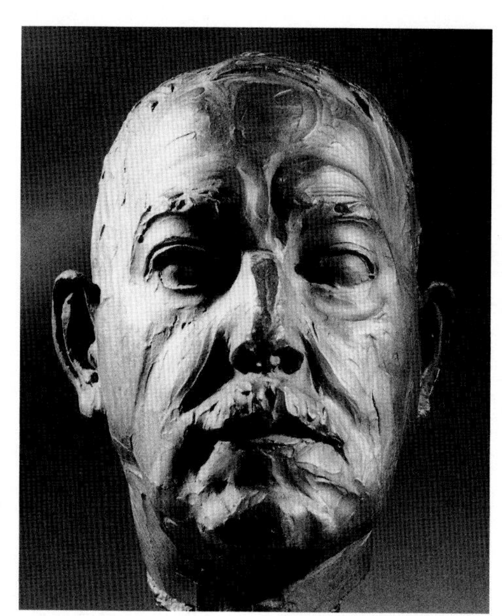

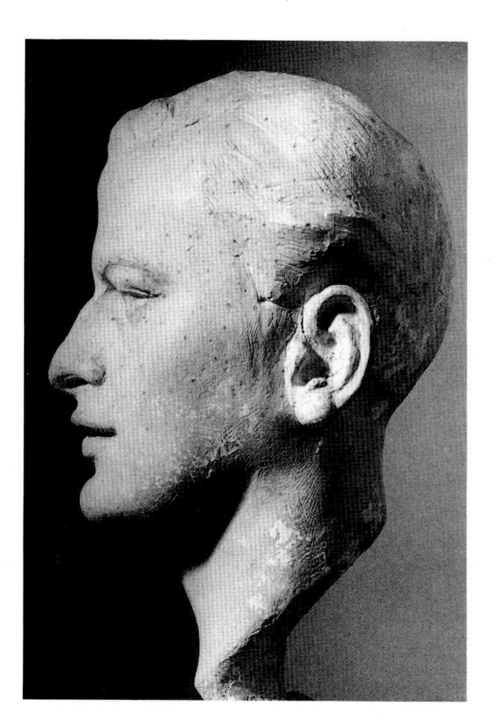
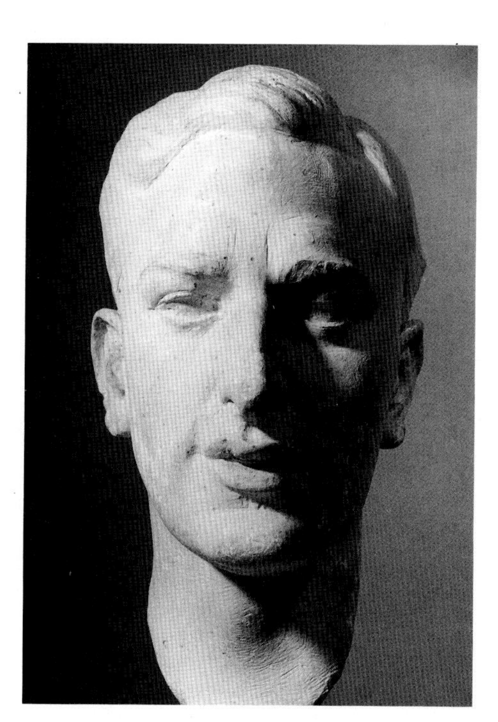
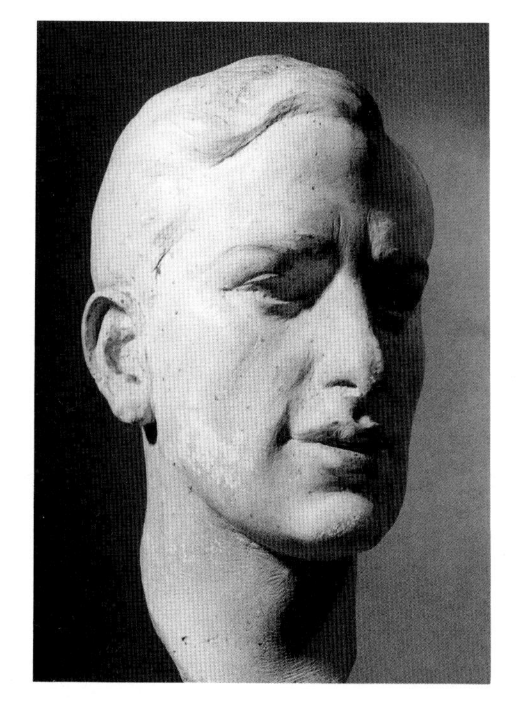

HEAD OF EDWARD M. M. WARBURG *1933*

CATALOG OF WORKS

Elevation, 1912-27
Bronze, 70 x 29 x 16 $^{3}/_{4}$ in.
The Lachaise Foundation, Boston
Salander-O'Reilly Galleries, New York
page 102

Elevation, 1912-27
Bronze, 70 x 29 x 16 $^{3}/_{4}$ in.
National Trust for Historic Preservation
Nelson A. Rockefeller bequest,
Pocantico Historic Property
page 108

The Biggest Little Woman in the World, c. 1918
Bronze, 11 $^{3}/_{4}$ in.
The Lachaise Foundation, Boston
Salander-O'Reilly Galleries, New York
page 110

Torso, 1927
Bronze, 6 $^{1}/_{2}$ x 7 x 3 $^{1}/_{2}$ in.
The Lachaise Foundation, Boston
Salander-O'Reilly Galleries, New York
page 111

Dancer, 1928
Bronze, 10 $^{3}/_{4}$ x 8 $^{3}/_{4}$ x 3 $^{1}/_{2}$ in., including base.
The Museum of Modern Art, New York
Gift of Abby Aldrich Rockefeller
page 114

Moment of Falling, 1928
Bronze, 13 x 12 $^{5}/_{8}$ x 4 $^{1}/_{2}$ in.
The Lachaise Foundation, Boston
Salander-O'Reilly Galleries, New York
page 116

Standing Nude, Left Hand Raised, 1927
Bronze, 11 $^{3}/_{4}$ x 5 $^{1}/_{2}$ x 2 $^{1}/_{2}$ in.
The Lachaise Foundation, Boston
Salander-O'Reilly Galleries, New York
page 118

Standing Nude, c. 1927
Bronze, 12 $^{1}/_{8}$ x 5 $^{1}/_{4}$ x 3 $^{1}/_{2}$ in.
The Metropolitan Museum of Art, New York
page 120

Classic Torso, 1928
Polished Bronze, 11 x 7 x 3 in.
The Iris & B. Gerald Cantor Collection
page 124

Head of a Girl, 1927
Tinted marble, 14 $^{1}/_{2}$ in. high, excluding original
Belgian black marble base
Hirschl & Adler Galleries, New York
page 125

Heroic Head, c. 1930-32
Bronze, 11 $^{3}/_{4}$ x 8 x 11 $^{3}/_{4}$
The Lachaise Foundation, Boston
Salander-O'Reilly Galleries, New York
page 128

Striding Woman, 1928-30
Bronze, 18 x 10 x 6 $^{1}/_{2}$ in.
The Lachaise Foundation, Boston
Salander-O'Reilly Galleries, New York
page 131

Torso, 1928
Bronze, 9 $^{1}/_{2}$ x 7 $^{3}/_{4}$ x 4 in.
The Lachaise Foundation, Boston
Salander-O'Reilly Galleries, New York
page 134

Torso, 1928
Bronze, 9 x 6 x 4 $^{1}/_{2}$ in.
The Lachaise Foundation, Boston
Salander-O'Reilly Galleries, New York
page 136

Reclining Woman, 1930
Bronze, 13 $^{1}/_{4}$ x 16 $^{3}/_{4}$ x 16 $^{1}/_{4}$
The Lachaise Foundation, Boston
Salander-O'Reilly Galleries, New York
page 138

Burlesque Figure, 1930
Bronze, 24 x 8 $^{1}/_{2}$ x 6 in.
The Lachaise Foundation, Boston
Salander-O'Reilly Galleries, New York
page 142

Breasts, Small, 1930
Bronze, 6 x 6 $^{1}/_{2}$ x 4 $^{1}/_{2}$ in.
The Lachaise Foundation, Boston
Salander-O'Reilly Galleries, New York
page 146

Seated Woman Holding Breasts, 1931
Bronze, 6 $^{1}/_{2}$ in.
The Lachaise Foundation, Boston
Salander-O'Reilly Galleries, New York
page 148

Torso, 1930-32
Bronze, 11 x 8 x 6 1/2 in.
The Lachaise Foundation, Boston
Salander-O'Reilly Galleries, New York
page 150

Abstract Figure, c. 1930-32
Bronze, 5 1/2 x 13 x 5 3/4 in.
The Lachaise Foundation, Boston
Salander-O'Reilly Galleries, New York
page 152

Man Walking (Portrait of Lincoln Kirstein), 1933
Bronze, 23 1/4 x 10 3/4 x 7 in.
Hirschl & Adler Galleries, New York
page 154

Man, 1938
Bronze, 8 ft. 4 in. (Plaster, 1930-35)
National Trust for Historic Preservation
Nelson A. Rockefeller bequest,
Pocantico Historic Property
page 157

Standing Woman, 1932
Bronze (cast 1932)
7' 4" x 41 1/8 x 19 1/8 in.
The Museum of Modern Art, New York
Mrs. Simon Guggenheim Fund.
page 160

Kneeling Woman, 1932-35
Bronze, 19 3/4 in.
The Lachaise Foundation, Boston
Salander-O'Reilly Galleries, New York
page 164

Passion, c. 1932-34
Bronze, 25 1/2 x 13 x 19 1/2 in.
The Lachaise Foundation, Boston
Salander-O'Reilly Galleries, New York
page 166

Standing Woman with Dark Head, c. 1930-35
Bronze, 18 x 8 3/4 x 4 1/2 in.
The Lachaise Foundation, Boston
Salander-O'Reilly Galleries, New York
page 170

Breasts, 1933
Marble, 8 x 7 3/8 x 5 1/4 in.
Collection of Edward M.M. Warburg, New York
page 173

Torso, 1933
Marble, 11 3/4 in.
Smith College Museum, Northampton, Massachusetts
page 176

Knees, 1933
Bronze cast 1946, with base, 16 x 13 3/4 11 1/2 in.
The Metropolitan Museum of Art, New York
page 180

Knees, 1933
Marble, 19 x 14 3/4 x 11 3/4 in., including base.
The Museum of Modern Art, New York
Gift of Mr. and Mrs. Edward M. M. Warburg
page 181

Female Figure (Torso), 1931
Aluminum, 12 x 8 1/4 x 4 1/2 in.
Philadelphia Museum of Art
Gift of George Howe
page 182

Torso, 1933
Bronze, 13 1/2 x 9 x 5 in.
The Lachaise Foundation, Boston
Salander-O'Reilly Galleries, New York
page 184

Kneeling Torso, Arms Outstretched, c. 1930-35
Bronze, 10 1/4 x 7 3/4 3 1/2 in.
The Lachaise Foundation, Boston
Salander-O'Reilly Galleries, New York
page 188

Large Nude with Hat, c. 1930-35
Bronze, 18 1/4 x 9 x 6 3/4 in.
The Lachaise Foundation, Boston
Salander-O'Reilly Galleries, New York
page 192

Kneeling Woman, Hands on Head, 1930-35
Bronze, 10 x 5 1/4 x 8 in.
The Lachaise Foundation, Boston
Salander-O'Reilly Galleries, New York
page 194

Dynamo Mother, 1933
Bronze, 11 1/8 x 17 3/4 x 7 1/4 in.
The Lachaise Foundation, Boston
Salander-O'Reilly Galleries, New York
page 198

In Extremis, 1934
Bronze, 15 x 10 1/4 x 9 1/2 in.
The Lachaise Foundation, Boston
Salander-O'Reilly Galleries, New York
page 201

Torso, c. 1930-35
Bronze, 12 3/4 x 5 x 5 3/4 in.
The Lachaise Foundation, Boston
Salander-O'Reilly Galleries, New York
page 204

Bust of Garden Figure, 1934
Bronze, 25 1/2 x 26 x 13 1/2 in.
The Lachaise Foundation, Boston
Salander-O'Reilly Galleries, New York
page 206

"Dans la Nuit," 1935
Bronze, 88 1/4 x 41 in.
National Trust for Historic Preservation;
Nelson A. Rockefeller bequest,
Pocantico Historic Property
page 209

Study for Standing Woman, 1934
Bronze, 17 x 8 3/4 x 5 3/4 in.
The Lachaise Foundation, Boston
Salander-O'Reilly Galleries, New York
page 212

Standing Woman, 1935
Bronze, 79 x 28 x 18 in.
The Lachaise Foundation, Boston
Salander-O'Reilly Galleries, New York
page 214

The Mountain, 1934-35
Bronze, 49 x 102 x 42 in.
The Lachaise Foundation, Boston
Salander-O'Reilly Galleries, New York
page 220

Torso with Arms Raised, 1935
Bronze, 37 x 33 1/2 x 16 1/2 in.
The Lachaise Foundation, Boston
Salander-O'Reilly Galleries, New York
page 224

Abstract Figure, c. 1935
Bronze, 16 1/2 x 10 x 11 1/4 in.
The Lachaise Foundation, Boston
Salander-O'Reilly Galleries, New York
page 228

Madame Lachaise in an Armchair (Portrait of the Artist's Mother), 1912
Plaster, 8 x 4 3/4 x 5 7/8 in.
The Metropolitan Museum of Art, New York
Bequest of Allys Lachaise
page 230

Portrait Bust of Lemuel Torrens, 1924
Bronze, 13 x 11 5/8 x 10 in.
Salander-O'Reilly Galleries, New York
page 233

Scofield Thayer, 1923
Bronze, 12 5/8 x 6 1/4 x 9 3/8
The Metropolitan Museum of Art, New York
Bequest of Scofield Thayer
page 234

Marianne Moore, 1924
Bronze with gold patina, 14 7/8 in.
The Metropolitan Museum of Art, New York
page 235

Head of Georgia O'Keeffe, 1927
Alabaster, 28 in.
The Metropolitan Museum of Art, New York
page 236

Henry McBride, 1928
Bronze, 13 5/8 x 10 1/8 x 11 1/8 in.
The Museum of Modern Art, New York
Gift of Maximilian H. Miltzlaff
page 238

John Marin, 1928
Bronze, 14 1/2 x 9 5/8 x 9 1/2 in.
The Museum of Modern Art, New York
Gift of Abby Aldrich Rockefeller
page 239

Head of Edward M. M. Warburg, 1933
Alabaster, 14 1/2 x 8 x 9 in.
The Metropolitan Museum of Art, New York
Gift of Edward M.M. Warburg
page 240

NOTES

1. *"Barbara Rose's Journal,"* Art & Auction *(March 1992), pp. 46, 48.*
2. *Barbara Rose, "Gaston Lachaise and the Heroic Ideal,"* Gaston Lachaise: Sculpture *(New York: Salander-O'Reilly Galleries, 1991), p. 14.*
3. *Louise Bourgeois, "Obsession"* Artforum 30 *(April 1992), p. 85.*
4. *Gaston Lachaise, "A Comment on My Sculpture,"* Creative Art *(August 1928), p. xxiii.*
5. *Donald Bannard Goodall, "Gaston Lachaise, Sculptor," Ph.D. diss., Harvard University, 1969, p. 350.*
6. *Gilbert Seldes, "Profiles: Hewer of Stone,"* New Yorker, *April 4, 1931, p. 28.*
7. *Lachaise,* Creative Art., *p. xxiii.*
8. *Gaston Lachaise, quoted in* Gaston Lachaise: Portrait Sculpture *(Washington D.C.: National Portrait Gallery, 1985), p. 7.*
9. *Gaston Lachaise to Pierre Christophe. May 1907, Lachaise Archive, Beinecke Library; cited in Gerald Nordland,* Gaston Lachaise: The Man and His Work *(New York: George Braziller, 1974) p. 12.*
10. *Marsden Hartley, from* Twice a Year *(Fall–Winter 1939), cited in* The Sculpture of Gaston Lachaise, *(New York: Eakins Press, 1967), p. 27.*
11. *Lachaise,* Creative Art, *pp. xxiii, xxvi.*
12. *Nordland,* Gaston Lachaise, *p. 4.*
13. *Ibid, p. 3.*
14. *Ibid, p. 4.*
15. *Cited in Nordland, Gaston Lachaise, p. 6.*
16. *Seldes, "Profiles," p. 29.*
17. *Nordland, Gaston Lachaise, pp. 6–7.*
18. *Roy Gordon Carter, quoted in Nordland, Gaston Lachaise, p. 9.*
19. *Isabel Lachaise, quoted in Nordland, pp. 9–10.*
20. *Seldes, "Profiles," p. 28.*
21. *Letter to Allys Lachaise from Mrs. Alice Chapman, quoted in Nordland, p. 11.*
22. *Lachaise, 1931 biography, pp. 25–26.*
23. *Ibid.*
24. *Lachaise, quoted in Nordland, Gaston Lachaise, p. 20.*
25. *Henry McBride,* Lachaise *(New York: Brummer Gallery, 1928), quoted in Nordland, Gaston Lachaise, pp. 21–22.*
26. *Barbara Rose, catalog essay, p. 10.*
27. *Ibid.*
28. *Seldes, "Profiles," p. 31.*
29. *Simone de Beauvoir, quoted in Dorothy Dinnerstein,* The Mermaid and The Minotaur: Sexual Arrangements and Human Malaise *(New York, 1977), p. 127.*
30. *Barry Schwabsky, "Shamelessness,"* Sculpture *(July–August 1992), p. 46.*
31. *Hartley, p. 28.*
32. *Cited in Sam Hunter and John Jacobus,* Modern Art: Painting, Sculpture, Architecture, (New York, *1985), p. 71*

NOTES